THE LIE

IRENE STRAYHORN

NEWMAN SPRINGS PUBLISHING
320 Broad Street
Red Bank, NJ 07701

First originally published by Newman Springs Publishing 2024

ISBN 979-8-89061-222-9 (Paperback)
ISBN 979-8-89061-223-6 (Digital)

Printed in the United States of America

CONTENTS

PREFACE

ost of the characters' names and the names of towns and states in this book have been changed to protect the innocence and privacy of those whom I had interactions with in my life. The purpose for my writing this book is to bring to light how a person can be delivered and set free from a lifelong struggle of being in bondage to the adversary, how that came to be, and the journey of breaking that stronghold over oneself to freedom and healing. It does not seem feasible that so many negative things can happen to one person throughout their life, yet so many terrible things happened that I had to recover from.

There is resolve, a way out from what seems to be impending doom with no escape. Unfortunately, many people never learn the truth of how their lives came to the place in which they find themselves. I hope and pray that those who go on this journey of my life with me in this book will be awakened and see the light at the other end of the tunnel. I pray this will bring hope to the hopeless and help to the helpless by taking this journey with me on roads many are and have traveled looking for something better, a way out. There is an open door awaiting you, leading to salvation and freedom.

My mission for life has been and still is to encourage abused, hopeless people to find their purpose in life and to instruct and inspire them to develop skills to be productive in society and in their spiritual walk. May you be blessed and helped in finding your way to freedom by this reading.

ACKNOWLEDGMENTS

T hank You, Adonai Yeshua and Ruach haKodesh, for commanding me to write this book and instructing me in the writing of it, including personal confessions, trials, tribulations, and successes and victories in my life's journey and my new awakening. The Lord's instructions were to write this book for others who are trapped, struggling, hurting, oppressed, or just plain sitting on the fence of life that they may find hope and encouragement of their own by coming on this journey with me. Blessed are You, Yehovah our God, Who heals all flesh and acts wondrously.

I want to thank my family, especially my daughter Elizabeth for her support in my writing of this book, for technical help as well as the final typing and editing. To the family—Rodney, William, Phillip, Matthew, Madeline, Oliver, Joy, Christopher, Natalie, and Cecily—for their wonderful patience when their mom, Elizabeth, was deep into the bowels of the book, unable to care for them at their beck and call. Truly, Elizabeth deserves the title of the "2020 Daughter of the Year."

Special thanks to Michelle and Joey Benami of Sukkat Shalom Jewish Messianic Congregation for reviewing this book and as a source of help in Freedom Ministry to all who are seeking a better life and freedom from bondage. May your dedication to bring love, joy, peace filled with blessing, and freedom touch every soul the Lord brings to you.

Thank you, Charlotte Barnes, for counseling and advice; Michelle Benami, Cynthia Peaslee, Deborah Lawson, and Mayoli Pascoe for previewing the book; Janet Stalvey for typing much of the preliminary manuscript. And I want to thank all of my friends and family of Sukkat Shalom whom the Lord has brought into my life who truly love me and have supported me through good and bad. You are all awesome and wonderful. Thank you for your dedication. You are truly awesome, compassionate, patient, and I look forward to reigning with you in heaven and the New Jerusalem in the future.

CHAPTER 1

Prelude

ooking out the window as I am sitting on my comfortable feather-filled sofa, I notice it has stopped raining, and the sky is gray and gloomy. My mind wanders back to the days of gloom and doom in my past. Having gone through journals I wrote long ago, I came upon one dated July 28, 1979 (I was at age thirty-seven remembering the past). Joseph died, so did mom, and so did I.

My brother Joseph died. I didn't see him when he was born, not until he was three months old. I was taken away to Europe for six months, and when I was brought back, Janie, my little sister, and mom Terri were living alone with Joseph. I fell in love with him right away, with his round cheeks and little fat body. He was fun to take care of, except for wringing out the diapers and cleaning off his hind end. He was soon left alone to explore and get into mischief like most kids do when not attended. I used to stay home from school every so often to be with him and babysit. He became my very own baby when I was only eleven years old.

Mom came home from the doctor one day very upset, nearly hysterical, crying, sobbing loudly, with another woman supporting her from behind. She blared out some unrealistic words like, "I am going to die," and frightened me. I could not believe what I was hearing and pretended I didn't hear anything. After many months of Mom crying, illnesses, and we kids living in different places, I became very depressed and angry.

One afternoon, Mom was in her bathrobe and listening to a song on the radio. "The shrimp boats are coming; there's dancing tonight." She started singing and suddenly jumped up and started dancing, taking Joseph's hand as she made her dance steps. It certainly shocked me to see a dying person jump up and do that when depression and gloom were ever present in Noni and Nono's house, where we were now living.

Shortly after that, just a matter of days, Mom disappeared from the house, and we were told she went to a hospital, then another one farther away into the big city (San Francisco)—too far for me to go see her and find her by myself. Why didn't she tell me or say goodbye? Who took her away?

Even though it was sunny and warm, a cold chill ran through me as I heard Noni and Nono shouting yet again. This day, though, was not at all typical. They were told Mom had died by one of her friends whom they hated. There were no immediate tears, just hate and horrible, disgusting words in the house. How could Mom leave us without saying goodbye and not telling me what to do?

I don't know what to do! I am only thirteen! I'm lost; she rejected me, left me alone to die all by myself in this house with Noni and Nono and Janie. I am so angry and hurt. I will never see her again. Nevertheless, I still have my brother, my baby Joseph. He loves me and needs me, and I need him.

Fester, Mom's last husband and father to Joseph, came and spoke to Nono and Noni. They decided Joseph should go back with Fester to Oklahoma. But they didn't ask me! I am his mother now! He belongs to me! You can't take him away from me. He's mine! But I had no choice—never did have. He was gone just as he had appeared suddenly in my life.

Mom shouldn't have allowed this to happen. It's all her fault. She left me, then Joseph was taken. He died just like Mom died. She was there, and then she wasn't. Joseph was there, and then he wasn't. I died. My life had ended just like that. Only things left are hatred, jealousy, the unknown, confusion, emptiness, loneliness, restrictions, mistrust, and suspicion. I can't listen. Stop! I have to escape this. I can't handle this. Help me. Get me out of here!

No! No, I'm thirteen now. I can do this. No, I can't!

Forlorn, hopeless, abandoned, and insecure were how I felt and all that was left for me at this point in my life. I know this is hard to read and understand, for I was depressed, controlled, suicidal, mentally unstable, and overwhelmed when I wrote it, and those feelings continued for most of my life. Because my mother was, unfortunately, unstable, I spent much of my childhood living with my grandparents Noni and Nono. So now begins the saga of my life from the very beginning before I was born.

CHAPTER 2

Immigrants

S itting at my dining room table, having just finished dinner with one of my oldest grandsons, I said to him, "I so appreciate you spending time with me and talking about everything and anything. You have no idea what this means to me spending time with you. Your noodle Alfredo is absolutely delicious—perfect! Thank you for thinking of me.

"I told you I was writing a book, an autobiography. I have been journaling since the mid '70s and have been reviewing the journals and would like to share with you some of my past since you are the only grandson that comes to visit me, spending a little of your precious time with me. I love it and appreciate you so much."

My grandson smiled, looking at me, and nodded to go ahead, a young man of few words. I proceeded with my story.

My grandparents were immigrants from Italy. They arrived in New York in 1904 as newlyweds. My grandfather Paolo, whom I called Nono, at age twenty had just gotten out of military service in Italy and married Edda, who was only fifteen years old, whom I always called Noni. After some time in New York, they moved westward to Pittsfield, Massachusetts, where my mother, Terri, was born. They had two children born after that, a boy named Marc, who died at age seven due to accident resulting in blood poisoning, and a girl whose name was never spoken, for it was said she was born Mongoloid and died before she was one year old. My grandparents never spoke much about their relatives or their two deceased children, but they did focus a great deal of attention on my mother, Terri—her negative side. I don't remember a single positive word spoken of her around the house during the years I lived with them.

Nono, my grandfather, was a seemingly kind, quiet, bald, and strong man—small in stature—from Castelnuvo Don Bosco near Torino, Italy. He was a very hard worker, tending to the garden every day years later at home in California, as I remember. He loved growing flowers and vegetables and keeping the yard neatly trimmed. His favorite flowers were carnations and a Crazy Shasta daisy—spectacular white show when planted thickly in a row in front of the new house.

His favorite color was pink. The house was pink. The kitchen was pink, and he wore pink dress shirts with his wool suits. He was a diabetic and took insulin injections every day on his own. Noni refused to do that for him.

Noni, my grandmother, came from the province of Asti in North Italy. She was born in a poor small village in the mountains of Capriolo near France, where I learned later many of the people back then practiced medieval witchcraft, really not understanding that that was what they were doing. They devoted much of their religious life to strict Roman Catholic rites, surely some of which they conjured up themselves.

She was a very unhappy woman, very bitter most of the time. When she tried to show happiness to demonstrate she was an okay person, it came off as fake. Most of the time, Noni would speak in Piedmontese, one of the many dialects in Italy. When Noni and Nono arrived in America, they brought with them their practices, what they knew.

Noni must have been a mischievous, rebellious person in her earlier years. One unusual day, she recounted to me that Nono had locked her out of their home back in Massachusetts one night. She said she went to a party by herself against his wishes or without his knowledge, and Nono was angry that she left leaving him home. When she returned, there was snow and ice on the ground, and she couldn't get in the house. It was very cold and started snowing again. Nono refused to open the doors. She slept outside and became ill and was hospitalized with pneumonia. She said she never forgave him for that. I recall her actions toward Nono were less than loving and kind all they days I was with them. She was not a forgiving person.

Terri, my mother, was born in 1912 to uneducated parents having only first- and third-grade educations. Terri felt trapped between this new modern world, English-speaking country, and the old-fashioned, discarded way of Italian country life her parents brought with them from the late 1800s. She was free-spirited and rebellious, wanting to live as Americans lived, not forced to do her parents' old-fashioned, discarded way of Italian life but her own way. Terri was talented and good-looking and had olive complexion, dark chestnut hair, and green eyes. She caught the eye of many men.

Eventually, they moved farther west to California, specifically San Francisco, in the mission district, where many Italians took refuge and opened up businesses and lived out their lives. They bought a three-story home, now called the famous Painted Ladies of San Francisco, with small backyards yet big enough to have a nice garden.

Noni and Nono were not reared to show love, truth, and compassion for the most part. Therefore, Terri did not get positive, loving attention from them, only harsh, strict, controlling words of discipline, always correcting her. She never got praise for anything. Certainly, she needed love and assurance. Terri lived through two wars and depressions, which influenced her life behaviors, wants, and needs. In 1941, she met my father, Benton, who was five years older than her, and had a turbulent romance with him in which I was conceived and born in California. He was a tall fair-skinned red-headed man with blue eyes and quite handsome in my opinion.

While we lived in San Francisco, my godmother Benita spent a lot of time visiting us since she was only a few houses away. She had always wanted Terri to marry her son, but Terri refused even though they had a short-lived affair together.

One day, we were all at Benita's house. I remember being shorter than the dining room table while I was standing watching them. I know this because everyone was seated around the table talking. It was dark in the room because they covered the windows and had very low lighting. There was a glass ball in the middle of the table, and they were all chanting something in English and Italian. The very large wooden table started to shake and move, but no one was holding on to it. They did not see me standing there until I called for Mommy. One of them rebuked me and told me to get out.

I heard this strange woman (a medium) at the end of the table calling for Benita's dead husband to come forth, and I turned and ran into the other room. It was frightening! I didn't like it at all and wanted to go home. This was my first real encounter with Satan— pure evil—and I never forgot the incident. I wonder now how often my parents participated in this evil.

My godmother Benita recounted to me when I was an adult that when I was a baby, the family was going on a train trip out of town. She was carrying me, and somehow, while getting on or off the train, she stumbled and dropped me out of the train to the ground. I often wonder if that is where I got the scars on the top side of my hands, or perhaps they were caused by Noni, who used a thick ruler to hit my hands, and those of the foster children if we did not obey her.

When I was three years old, I remember being in the back seat of a very large Packard, picking up my half sister Janie from the hospital. Apparently, she was born ill and had whooping cough and some other illness and was kept at the hospital for three months. My mother, Terri, came to the car with this little baby wrapped up in a blanket. She showed me the bundle, and I lifted my hand to touch her face and hands. Noni yelled at me, slapping my hand sharply, and said "Don't touch her. You will make her sick."

I was so hurt that I reclined backward into the seat and sulked. I decided I didn't like this baby Janie or any of these big people. I didn't want to hurt her, but now I didn't want to have anything to do with her, and I decided to stay away from her and these older people. I went into a shell.

"Grandson, can you believe this?" When we lived in San Francisco in the three-story house with a basement, my grandparents became foster parents with the county for pay. They were given several smaller children around the age of Janie and me, between one and five years of age. I remember her yelling at us, the children, to sit on the floor of the kitchen, and she would hand each one of us food in a bowl, making me feel like I wasn't worth enough to sit in a chair.

One of the girls, slightly older than me, got tired of it, and she conspired with me to run away. I was afraid to say no and afraid to say okay because of Noni's mean temper, but one day, I ran away with her. We didn't get very far. The big black-and-white police car drove us back to the house to a very mad, snorting old lady called Noni! Shortly after that, all the children were gone and never came back. My grandparents sold the house and moved farther south in what was called the Bay Area after some time had gone by.

Nono, being a carpenter, enjoyed and did carpentry work like building a two-story house on two acres in the country off an old highway, which is now a busy big freeway in a big metropolitan area prior to moving into a town. The acreage was turned into a trailer park after he sold it, but while we lived there—that is, my grandparents, my half sister, and myself—they farmed the land. They had livestock and chickens and grew over an acre of wheat. When the wheat was ready for harvesting, Nono got out his huge long-handled sickle and would swing it back and forth, cutting the long stalks. Noni walked behind him, picking up the cut stocks and placing them in her very large apron. They had a place where they would shake the stocks to harvest the seed, then the stocks were piled about ten feet high. They allowed my sister and me to climb up on the top of the mound and slide down. That was one of the very few treats we got to do as children.

In 1948, we were still living there when there was a large-scale earthquake that shook the building violently. All of us were sleeping upstairs, and our beds started moving and sliding around the room, scaring us while we were sitting in the beds, looking around in wonder and fear. That's the first experience I had with earthquakes that

I can remember, which are very common in California. No damage was done to this two-story house.

When Noni made her big meals for company on holidays for friends and relatives, she changed her character to being very festive and happy, drinking lots of red wine, vermouth, and other alcoholic beverages. I remember several lit candles on the table with an array of wine bottles. Dinners took several hours. By the time dessert came around, the adults were pretty inebriated. Then came the espresso. By this time, Noni would be snorting cigarette smoke out of her nostrils, acting very foolish for attention in front of everyone.

On one occasion, my mother, Terri, had her husband, Dave, present, along with her ex-husband and his new wife at the same table, exchanging weird looks at one another, along with unexplainable speech toward one another. When the party was over and everyone was gone, Noni would begin the bashing, cursing comments toward everyone she found displeasure with. That's when I would learn things about people I would not be told at any other time.

Most of my childhood, I spent with my grandparents, totally resenting it due to their unforgiving ways and negative speech and meanness toward me. The few times I stayed with Terri, life was difficult because she never had enough money for necessities, never mind the fact that I watched her being beaten by husbands, men in general, and even her parents with excessive yelling. Plus, I always seemed to end up doing the dishes, dusting, and cooking. Ugh!

When I was ten, Terri was pregnant with her third child, but it wasn't being discussed in the family. My grandparents decided to take a six-month trip to Italy and France to see their relatives so as not to be around when Terri gave birth. They made arrangements to take me with them. It was planned so Terri would not have me around to help her with the newborn, but I was totally unaware of that fact. We boarded a huge ship in New York and headed for Europe. We had taken a train to New York and slept on top of our luggage between the seats, which was very uncomfortable. However, our rooms on the ships going there and coming back were really nice.

I was given freedom to walk around the entire ship alone. Sometimes it got really spooky way down under in the pool area—

dark and misty, like fog—bringing thoughts of monsters waiting for me. But I had fun looking in the shops and walking around the library on this French line called *Liberté*. This was the first freedom I ever experienced in my life. I loved being left alone for a while and being on the water.

We landed in Le Havre, France, and toured around that country, first visiting Nono's relatives who lived there. To my surprise, Nono spoke fluent French with them while Noni sat listening, trying to be noticed. Seeing the Eiffel Tower in Paris was awesome to me even at ten years old about to turn eleven.

Nono purchased a Fiat car, and while we were driving one day in Italy on a rural country road, my grandparents were conversing about the possibility of running into Gypsies who had taken over someone's land and orchard, for several bands of Gypsies had seized others' properties. They debated what to do to escape from being robbed and killed, scaring me completely.

Suddenly we came upon a hit-and-run accident. A man was lying on the road, severely injured and bleeding. His Vespa was totally smashed a few feet away. Noni argued to leave him there and turn the car around so no one would think we hit him. Nono finally, angrily, gave in and turned the car around and drove off in the direction we came, leaving this injured, possible dying man crumpled on the road. I was heartsick and could not understand this action. I hated Noni's decision and decided they were cowards and terrible people. They made me feel guilty, too, like I was a bad person. I never forgot the incident.

My six-month stay in Europe was as interesting as it could get for a now-eleven-year-old girl. I met very different people from what I had known. They, most of them, had lots of money, dressed very well, owned businesses, etc. We stayed in one of their hotels in the big city of Torino. Up until then, I never saw such a beautiful hotel, which had marble floors and steps. They had money!

I was sent to the room a lot while adults conversed, but I enjoyed looking out the window, watching and listening to bicycle rings and auto horns barking down below. I liked this different atmosphere. To this day, the sounds of the city are attractive to me. The food that was served was always delicious to me, and I ate to my heart's content. The music was very Latin with lots of polka dancing, which I loved.

Somehow, my grandparents seemed to have money they appeared not to have before. Nono ordered a horse-drawn carriage for us to tour Torino in style, and they bought expensive items they would not purchase at home. Nono paid cash for the Fiat car we drove around during the six months there. They almost brought it home but decided against it because of shipping costs. They purchased two Necchi sewing machines, one for Terri and the other to keep, and shipped them home, along with many other items.

We visited some of Noni's relatives in a very rural area of northern Italy. They lived in a broken-down house and were raising giant pigs that seemed taller than me. I was warned not to go near them, for they would not hesitate to eat me! Really…perhaps just a ploy to control my presence?

We came back on an American ship line called *Independence*, which I enjoyed a lot also. I loved being on the water and feeling the wind in my face when I was on the deck.

When we finally got back to America, I went back to Terri's house and started school. First day back, the teacher introduced me as a kid from Italy. I almost forgot English, and the students made fun of me. I had gained weight from all of the rich food, which we consumed in large quantities in Europe, and had a bit of a protruding round stomach. The boys would make fun of me by walking with their stomachs pushed out, laughing. That was so hurtful and embarrassing. I became a loner and did not want to eat anything anymore. But I did anyway—even more.

Feelings of rejection and ugliness overwhelmed me and left a lifetime scar. By this time, my half brother Joseph was three months old, and Janie had been taking care of him. I very promptly took over the job, remembering how *all* my parents favored Janie over me. I wasn't going to let her have fun with this baby! He was so cute and chunky.

Terri was sick a lot, so I stayed home often to babysit Joseph. The realization of smelly, stinky, dirty diapers sunk in, and it wasn't so fun anymore. The same stepdad Fester did not like me at all and was always commanding me to wash the dishes, cook dinner, vacuum the living room, etc. I was afraid of him, having seen how he treated my mother. He always favored Janie over me. I never knew why. Perhaps it was because she had the dark hair and complexion as my mother while I was very fair.

Noni did have some very good qualities and talents as I discovered while living with her. She was a very good cook, from whom I learned much from observation, for she would not let anyone help her in preparing food. I learned enough from her that in my adulthood, I was able to prepare seven-course meals in the traditional Italian style.

Noni was also a good seamstress in early life and crocheted many afghans and fine small items. She excelled in needlepoint and embroidery, which I also learned and loved to do. But when it came to taking care of my half sister Janie and me, she was mean and very strict. We were only allowed to bathe once a week, and it had to be in a tub because showering wasted so much water and could not be used again. So we all took turns bathing in the same bath water. Many times she would scoop the water out with a bucket and pour it in the garden until it was too difficult to retrieve. The remaining water would go down the drain.

We had to stand next to the gas floor furnace to get our hair dry and stay warm. The heater was used sparingly to save money. However, they would open the oven door and turn the oven on to heat the kitchen and dining room. Of course it was also gas. Apparently, they thought that was a cheaper way to go. Janie and I did not have anything called *playtime.*

"So, Grandson, that was just a part of my beginnings and what my grandparents were like and how my mother lived when I was growing up," I said.

He acknowledged without words, seemingly in shock, and gave me a good hug then left for home since the hour was late. I continued to ponder about the past encounters of my life reflecting back to my mother, Terri, which we will get into in the next chapters.

CHAPTER 3

My Mother's Rebellion

My mother, Terri, was tormented by her parents all the time. They never let up. I remember living on Flynn Avenue when I was little and later in elementary school. My grandparents flew into the house yelling and started hitting her. They were *reprimanding* her for yet another intolerable thing she had done. Weeping, she ran to escape from their abuse while I looked on. Mother was not able to handle any relationship or marriage but kept looking for love in all the wrong places. I was left with Noni and Nono much of the time. Terri had many jobs that didn't last. She even had a corset shop that her parents provided for her. It didn't last. Nothing took hold.

I do remember that I was left home alone a lot to watch TV. To my misfortune, very scary monster movies were always on the TV, and I was too scared to get off the sofa to turn it off or change the black-and-white channel. I just knew if I put my leg or foot down to the floor, a monster was going to devour me, and I'd be dead or eaten alive. All these memories came back to haunt me when I was an adult on my own.

Tragically, Terri was unable to take care of us children most of the time. She was either sick, working full-time, looking for work, or finding a new husband. Noni and Nono raised us children very strictly without tenderness and love so necessary for a child to develop into caring human beings. Whenever my mother had us children with her, we would end up sleeping in the back seat of her car while she was in the bars, or we stayed with strangers who felt put upon and let us know with few words and disgusting looks. They seemed to feel sorry for us and at the same time did not want to be involved with us.

Terri had many encounters with various men, as told by Noni in her conversations with her friends. She had been married six times, according to Noni, and had an abortion of a male child before I was conceived, for she was not married at the time, it was said because Noni and Nono did not approve of Benton, her lover at the time I was conceived. They were not married, so she looked to abort me as well.

Fortunately, Benton had never been married and had no previous children. His conscience would not allow Terri to go through with an abortion. He married my mother in October of 1941 despite the wholly hostile opposition of her parents. My dad had gotten out of the military and became a butcher who shamefully had rolled into town on a boxcar as a stowaway, according to Noni, and a drunkard at that. Yet he took responsibility for his actions. Months later after I was born in 1942, they were divorced due to Noni and Nono's tormenting insistence and interference.

Benton's parents were so poor that as a young seven-year-old boy, they gave him away to an orphanage, for they had too many children to feed as destitute farmers. Benton never got over the rejection and abandonment for the rest of his life. He was never adopted but grew up in the orphanage. He most likely started drinking to drown his sorrows as soon as he was on his own.

Terri was not able to be a mother, but she did the best she could with limited knowledge and no affirmation. She was a child controlled and dominated by Noni. She always felt trapped and was punished all her life for my birth. I was a mistake! She suffered not only for my birth but those of my sister and brother by different men. Rebellion overpowered her. She finally died in shame, rejection, and abandonment. I never really got to know her, except by observation mostly. We did not hold mother-daughter talks/conversations, but I could see and feel her pain, suffering, and lack. This attitude, this spirit, fell upon me and stayed with me for most of my years until I was actually led by the Spirit of God to a church leader who was setting people free from their past in 2018.

I remember a time when my mother came home with Janie and me, cautiously going into the house then bedrooms, as though she was afraid someone might be hiding. She looked under the bed, all around the room suspiciously, then opened the closet door.

One time, out flew this angry man who started beating her up, and she fell backward onto the bed. He was hitting her continuously. I fled the room and hid somewhere. I don't remember the outcome that time, but I always felt fear of being next to get beaten up simply because I was my mother's unwanted, unloved, shameful, good-for-nothing female child. I never heard any of the family speak about the "God who loves us."

Another time, her last husband was at home. I was in my bed, and my sister was asleep in hers in the same room. I heard my mother screaming and her husband, Fester, yelling at her. I ran to her room, opened the door, and found her being dragged off the bed by her long dark hair by Fester. He was extremely angry and pulling her around the floor by her hair. He saw me and yelled at me to get out while my mother screamed at me to call the police. I was scared for my life. "If you call the police," he yelled, "I will kill you next." I ran back to my room and jumped into bed to hide under the covers, waiting for his heavy footsteps in horror.

Another time, Fester was angry at my mother for something. Apparently, she had gone to a bar for a while without him. They got into a fight when she got home. Yelling ensued. She ran out the front door and across the street, heading for a field with Fester racing after her in the car, jumping the curb to run her over as I was watching from the living room window in terror. I still can't remember what happened—too much trauma for a child to bear. I retreated back to monster movies on TV.

My worst memory of Terri is seeing her tormented, yelled at, and hit by my grandmother and men. Hearing and seeing her crying out to stop always made me run away from the scene. I was always afraid of my grandparents and hated them for being so cruel and hateful to my mother and Janie…and myself! I believed all the lies of the devil spoken through my grandparents and mother. This is how the devil works to destroy families, but we (I) had no idea or understanding of this, for that matter anything spiritual.

The best memory I have of my mother is when I was eleven or twelve years old, seeing her in the kitchen having coffee at the breakfast table when I came back from Italy. She loved coffee with cream, sugar, and butter while smoking one cigarette after another. The house was always full of smoke. For my breakfast, she would give me the same beverage with toast or a doughnut before going to school. At times, she taught me how to sew dresses for my Vogue dolls, which started my love for sewing and designing clothes. She also taught me how to bake, which I did a lot of and still do. My favorite thing to bake was a banana nut bread, which we both loved, and I still do as an adult.

Terri loved music, singing, and dancing even when she was ill with leukemia. In her last days, she lived for six months alone in some hospital in San Francisco. Noni and Nono never went or took us to see her during that time. I often wonder now if she was saved, if she ever came to know the Lord and His love for her. Would she have been able to believe He loved her?

My grandparents had put curses on every one of their children, including us, their grandchildren. One by one, all their children died early, leaving only myself and Janie, who has been suffering with an illness for years. At Terri's funeral, my grandmother forced me to go look at my mother lying in a casket. When we got close, she put her hand on my head and shoved my face onto this cold dead body that did not look like my mother. It was scary, humiliating, and hateful to me.

I did not cry because of all the very distant Italian relatives who showed up that generally never came to visit. I just wanted to run away from them all. I was very angry at everyone there looking at me with scornful faces. I saw them as hypocrites and liars. They were secretly talking to each other about Janie and me while giving us the evil eye. A Children Services agent, a woman, came to visit us and gave me an old ladies broach to pacify me, further insulting me—a meaningless gift.

As time went on, now at age thirteen, I only concerned myself with ways of escaping and hurting people who hurt me. If I was not self-centered, I became concerned with self only and became an introvert. Helplessness and hopelessness were all I felt, unable to do anything about the cruelty imposed upon me, and I had no concern for my sister's welfare at that time, only myself since my brother Joseph was taken away from me shortly after my mother's death and funeral. No one consulted me or cared that I had deep feelings toward my half brother and wanted him with me. They just took him away without even saying goodbye. Again, a broken heart!

CHAPTER 4

Innocence Lost

Not long after my mother's death, my grandparents told me my alcoholic father, Benton, was coming to meet me. We picked him up at the train station. He showed up drunk and smelled of liquor just as they were anticipating in the car on the way to the station. My grandmother pushed me to him to hug this strange, smelly man and demanded I hug him. It was more than awkward since we never met before. My mother never told me I had a father of my own. She never talked about him. He was nonexistent. Now this strange man claims to be my father?

My grandparents took him back home with us, and he stayed three or four days. They had him sleep in the bed right next to mine in the same room where Janie and I slept. The next morning, he asked me if I always cry at night. I had no idea I cried during the night. He looked at the veins in my arms and my features to see if I was really his daughter, for he apparently had doubts. When it was time for him to leave, he said he could not take me with him, for his wife would not understand. Perhaps she knew nothing about me or his life before they were married. I will never know.

I didn't see him again until I graduated from high school, and he made another surprise visit. By this time, I was taller and thin and attractive. The visit was short and again he said he couldn't take me with him but sternly gave me advice not to lose any more weight. He loved my hair, for it was red, as his was—strawberry blonde, he called it. Benton was truly an alcoholic and still smelled of liquor. My grandparents had hoped he would take me off their hands the first time he came to visit. He had been writing me letters all along, but they were intercepted by Noni and Nono. I never saw any of them. He asked if I had gotten his letters and why I didn't I write back. I didn't know what to believe. People lie all the time at home, school, even neighbors. Who was I to believe him or them anyway?

Several years later, when I was married, I got an invitation to visit him and his new wife in Arizona, where he had been living. He was very happy, but his health was failing. He asked if I would leave my husband and come stay with him to get to know one another and take care of him. I flatly said no! How dare this man try to take control of my life after all these years. I felt sorry for him.

I never saw Benton again until two weeks before his death in 1983. He was in a VA hospital with organ damage due to alcohol abuse. I flew to his hometown to visit and sang hymns to him and some of the other patients in the VA hospital for those two days. His ashen face suddenly had color and a smile when he saw me and recognized who I was. We were both happy to see each other and conversed a little. He asked me to stay in his hotel room where he had been living. It was full of evil, familiar spirits that kept me awake. I hated it. Then I said my *goodbye* as my time was up. He died two weeks later.

I never went to his funeral or asked where they placed him. I never got to know him but sensed his emotional pain and suffering, his feeling of abandonment and rejection. It was like an aura around him. He believed all the lies of the devil, and believing and acting on those lies took him to his death. He was only in his midsixties.

Unfortunately, I believed all the lies told to me of my father and was unable to develop a relationship with him during his life. Fortunately, at the hospital, he had been open to discussing spiritual matters. Depending on what religion his wives practiced (he married two or three times after Terri), he simply went along with their beliefs. He allowed me to lead him in the prayer of salvation before I left the hospital. Only the Lord knows his heart and whether he is truly saved. I look forward to meeting him again in God's heavenly kingdom. How wonderful that would be for us if God allows it.

An incident that left me scarred for life happened by the hands of Noni after Terri's death and after my father, Benton, left. I was thirteen years old, getting ready to go into the eighth grade, still losing weight due to the trauma of losing my mother and being placed in my grandmother's home permanently by court order. It was late spring, and Noni had both Janie and me go outside into the backyard and line up in front of her. Nono was outside taking care of the garden as usual, his favorite pastime. He looked and probably wondered what Noni was up to. She demanded Janie and I take off our tops, literally strip naked to the waist, pulling at our tops.

I was mortified. Nono is out there! Neighbors can see us! But my fear of what she might do was greater than any humiliation I would have to bear. We stripped down, and the next thing I knew, she was sucking on our breasts all the while pretending to be a baby crying for milk. It was awful! She kept it up for a while, and I felt like I wanted to crawl into a hole and die.

This abuse later interfered with my womanhood. I didn't want anyone to touch me. Nono saw what she was doing and didn't do anything. He just kept on working in the garden as though it was nothing. I wonder now if this is what my grandmother was subjected to in Italy as a child or young woman and thought it was normal. How awful and devastating this practice would be for any child to experience.

When I was fourteen, another unfortunate incident occurred with my grandmother Noni. I was in the bathroom when suddenly, there was a mass of blood all over me, and I screamed, for I became so frightened. Noni came running in and knew exactly what happened but refused to tell me. Instead, she cursed me and said now I am really in trouble and was going to cause her and myself much trouble for the rest of my life. She left me sitting there and came back in the room with a bunch of ripped-up rags used for dusting and said to use that in my underwear, leaving me to figure it out on my own.

I couldn't imagine what sin I committed that God would hurt me and make me bleed. I ended up getting sick a lot, and they eventually had to take me to a doctor. He explained the monthly period process, and when he asked what protection I used, I told him my grandmother gives me old strips of rags. He became irate and ripped into Noni and totally embarrassed her. Needless to say, I was punished for speaking out of turn when I got home. When I got into high school PE classes, I felt embarrassed to undress and put PE clothes on.

While living with my grandparents during my high school years, Nono would drive to various Purity Grocery Stores and rummage through dumpsters. He was always fortunate to get a good supply of discarded food to take home and eat. I would slink down in the back seat of the car so no one would see me. It seemed embarrassing to me then, and I did not want to be made fun of at school. The food always looked and tasted good to me once it was prepared and served. We never got sick. Noni and Nono saved a lot of money doing this, and at their death, they left an estate of 350,000 dollars for Terri's three children when we arrived at a specific age. Unfortunately, most of the funds were lost by executors and lawyers or eaten up in taxes before distribution.

The years I lived with Nono and Noni along with Janie, my half sister, Noni would use fear to control us and keep us in line with their demands. They used tactics like, "A child-eating man dwells in the sewer system, and if you get too close to the drainage hole, he will reach out and grab you and pull you down into the sewer and eat you." I never went close to the sewer intakes even as an adult. Of course I believed them.

Another fable they used was telling us, "There are demons and monsters lurking outside the windows at night, so don't go close to the windows in the evenings, or they will grab you and pull you through and devour you." I often wondered as an adult if my mother used to sneak out the windows at night to go dancing, and they used this scare tactic to keep us in. I was fearful washing dishes in front of the kitchen window or sitting near a window at night my entire life until I received Jesus as my Lord and Savior in Hawaii in my forties.

When Noni, Janie, and I would go into town to shop, she kept her head down, looking at the sidewalk. She quite often found paper money lost on the ground, like one-hundred-dollar bills. It seemed she was embarrassed to look at people in the face. One time, a black person, male, was walking toward us on the sidewalk, and she grabbed both Janie and me by the arm and made us cross the street to the other sidewalk to avoid coming close to this black man. She was either very fearful or filled with hate and refused to go near him, uttering some degrading comments toward him. From that incident, I picked up the message we were to stay away from black people.

For several years, Noni had me washing my clothes by hand in the sink until they got a wringer washer, which I was able to master quickly. When not doing homework or household chores, she taught me how to embroider, to crochet afghans and scarves and some sewing. When it came to cooking, it was hands off, for she was in charge of the kitchen. I watched her make all kinds of complicated but tasty meals, which I memorized to make them myself someday. Raviolis took several days to make from scratch. She would take several kinds of meat and grind it up in a hand grinder and add garlic cubes, green herbs, tomatoes, onions, and finally add a few eggs to the mix. Then she carefully took a teaspoonful of the mix and place it on the hand-rolled dough she made the day before, strategically in a line, then turning the dough over it and cutting them with a handheld cutting implement. The sauce was always fresh tomatoes from the garden simmered in butter and garlic. We could hardly wait to eat them!

My grandparents would not buy us new clothes for school or holidays. They had to be used clothing, including shoes. Either the shoes were too small in size or too large. In which case, they would stuff the ends or top of the shoes with cloth pieces. The smaller shoes caused my feet to look like or become hammertoes. Noni decided to remedy that by putting half-inch iron rings on my toes, causing them to bleed and making it painful to walk. That was very embarrassing in high school. I kept it to myself and walked slowly.

Noni would buy material so I could learn how to make my own clothes, which I did. I signed up for sewing classes in high school and excelled in all those classes, even getting awards and certificates of accomplishment for sewing. I was asked to model what I made in a fashion show.

When either Janie or I were sick growing up, Noni would give us hot red wine with lemon and honey in it and put a hot brick wrapped in red cloth (to keep evil spirits away) at the foot of our bed to keep our feet warm. Many times, we would end up with a mustard plaster on our chest. I would lie on my pillow and pray the Lord God would take my life, although I was not sure what He would do with it. Beyond these few incidents, my high school years were only endured until I could get old enough to leave. I did not spend time with Janie, for she was four years behind me in school, and we did not have same interests and resented the better care they gave her over me.

High school was not much fun for me because of restrictions Noni and Nono imposed upon the activities in which I could participate. It was an escape from home, but while I was actually on school property and in classes, I had other problems to deal with, like fitting in. Because I was so sheltered at home from the outside world—except for TV shows like *I love Lucy*, wrestling, *Lawrence Welk Show*, and the news—I was easily shocked at the behavior and language of many of the other kids. I was so far removed from the worldly scene that whoever befriended me at school, I would try to be just like them. If they cursed and swore, then so did I, even if I wasn't sure what I was saying. If they cut classes, so did I, thinking I was just as clever as them. If they were straitlaced and frowned upon such behavior, then I would say I agreed with their thinking and tried to be upright in all things. I really needed someone to really like me and take an interest in me. Not believing in myself or even knowing who I was or what I believed in was perplexing and devastating to me.

Not having anyone to help me with the homework was hard. I just got by. English was the hardest subject because we spoke Italian at home. One semester, I ended up in a *dummies* class with the misfits of the school. How embarrassing. There was a determination in me that made me work harder not to fall into that trap again. Truly, I did not want to be identified as a troubled problem student (even if I was). I didn't want to fit into the lies my grandmother said I was destined for. It ended up that I was an average *C* student but excelled in the arts, sewing, and Italian language, getting mostly *A* grades in those classes. My grandmother had me writing letters to her relatives in Italy in Italian just as she dictated them.

One time, in my sophomore year, a very sweet, quiet boy came up to me and asked if he could carry my books to class for me. No one had shown any interest in me, and I was so pleased and surprised. I said yes, and he proudly took my books and walked me to class. He was a black boy and was ever so sweet and respectful. When I told my grandmother about it, I thought I'd never hear the end of it. She warned me to stay away from "that kind," or I would have hell to pay.

Fear gripped me, and I decided to end any kind of friendship with the boy immediately. The next day, I refused him without explanation, and he walked away brokenhearted, or so it appeared. It took me years to get over the fear instilled in me regarding the black race. I had no idea we were all sisters and brothers as the Word of God tells us until much later in life.

My junior year, I was invited to the senior prom by one of the seniors, an athlete named Ricky, who had been watching me secretly at school for some time. He had sent a friend of his over to me to question me if I would go out with his friend Ricky. I didn't much care for this person, who seemed to be a troubled kid. But after much conversation, I said I just might.

Eventually, Ricky introduced himself to me and said he would like me to meet his parents before going to the prom so they would know whom he was taking out. The night we drove back from meeting his parents on our way to my grandparents, we were hit by a speeding car, which ran the red light. The car we were in was totaled. Ricky passed out with a severe brain concussion, and my head went out through the side window and back in, making cuts to my face and head all the way to the bone.

I woke up in the emergency room of a hospital with doctors cutting my bloody sweater off while hearing my grandparents cursing and yelling at me in the background, saying I was a troublemaker and no telling what I had done to cause the accident. After many stitches to my face and head, I was sent home with my arm in a sling, nursing a cracked collar bone and multiple contusions. I wanted to stay in the hospital away from Noni, but it was not to be. Her Italian doctor did a great job stitching me up but was believing the lies about me Noni was spewing out of her mouth.

After a few days recovering at home, my grandparents were taking me to the doctor for a follow-up visit. As we were getting into the car, a vehicle from a florist shop pulled up and said he had flowers for me. I took them, but Nono grabbed the box out of my hand and said I didn't need any damn flowers. They were a dozen red roses from Ricky and his parents. Nono was so hurtful to me that I went into a shell and did not want to come out.

A few weeks later, Ricky recovered, and we were both back in school and seeing each other at school since I wasn't allowed to date or see him. After he graduated, he enlisted in the navy and wrote letters to me, saying he wanted to marry me when he got out. Knowing it was hopeless for me, I never responded and never saw him again. I learned a few years later, he became a carpenter and eventually had his own business. To this day, I have never forgotten him and his kindness and love for me and longed to see him again and wondered from time to time about his life's outcome.

There were some pleasures in life that I still love to this day. From age eleven, I loved art and did well at drawing composition. In high school, I loved to design and sew clothes, and it was fascinating to use all kinds of mediums in painting and crafts in the art classes. As an adult, I have pursued and enjoyed oil painting and sold many pieces of art. In my high school years, I dreamed of designing my own clothes and having my own dress shop, but as an adult, I just wanted to do oil paintings for fun, commission, and resale. From time to time, I made and designed articles of clothing for myself and others. However, some women got so persnickety that I gave up making clothes for others altogether. It just wasn't worth the agitation they put me through.

Now, as I have matured *somewhat* into a senior citizen, I can look back and understand why my grandparents were inclined that way. That's all they knew—how they were brought up in Italy. That's how my mother was brought up under my grandparents' care even though she rebelled against them. Terri had no good example, nor did she have God, Jesus, or the Holy Spirit. I can only imagine what horrible lives they had and why my grandparents escaped from their villages to come to America to have a better life. There was so much hidden from me—never spoken of or dealt with—during their lives and mine. I never knew to ask questions about their past and why they lived the way they did. So much unknown.

I learned a lot of good things from them through those difficult years that I apply to my life today. The Lord is so gracious to save. Terri learned much good from them also, such as cooking and sewing. She was an excellent seamstress and cooked fabulous meals around holidays. Even though we did not have a close relationship, I still missed her. The idea that has stuck with me through the years is responsibility, respect, and accountability, which they tried to teach me but did not give me. I longed for respect and love, and they seemed to have hidden that and themselves from me. These are so lacking in this world today. I had to learn the hard way as so many do in this age.

CHAPTER 5

Early Single Life

A few months after I graduated from high school in 1960, I found a way to escape my grandparents' house. My girlfriend Daphne and I made up an elaborate story (a big fat lie) to get my grandparents out of the house for a few hours so I could pack my stuff and run away with Daphne. I called some Italian friends of theirs and asked them to invite my grandparents over to their home so I could prepare a surprise party for them while they were gone. They accepted to do so and invited my grandparents to their home for several hours, after which, they returned home to find me gone. Daphne had rented an apartment to which we both moved.

I was afraid of what might happen to me for this action when my grandparents found out. I was still in their control and in fear of them. There was much trembling inside of me and guilt, so I found it hard to enjoy my escape.

The first night in the apartment, Daphne had her boyfriend come over and spend the night with her. That was very scary to me because of what my grandmother said was forbidden and evil, and the next morning, I told her I didn't like her actions (because it was an unthinkable thing to do, and it scared me). Within a few days, I moved out since she thought nothing of having him there with her, but there was nowhere to go. I ended up back with my grandparents, to my utter dismay and fear.

Needless to say, I suffered the price for my actions and lies to my grandparents and their friends. There were daily reminders in insulting bashing language that I was exactly what they said I was, a troublemaker, no good for anything, just like my mother. I was not trusted and ridiculed in front of their friends and now having to sleep on the couch in the living room.

Daphne and I remained friends. A few months after high school graduation and running away from home, Daphne and I both entered a small-city beauty pageant without telling my grandparents, and we ended up in the local newspapers, along with the other contestants, wearing only a full-body swimsuit and high heels. It made us feel really good about ourselves for a very brief time. It was a wake-up call. Neither of us won, but I was able to see the corruption behind the scenes and decided I didn't want any part of that kind of lifestyle after all. I kept newspaper clippings of me on the event and felt important for a very brief time. My grandparents never found out, to my knowledge. I sent a newspaper clipping to my father and received no response.

Daphne had an older brother, Will, whom I was introduced to earlier. Daphne and her parents did not tell me he had been in and out of juvenile hall and lastly, jail. He had just been released and was back home with his parents. They wanted him out of their house. Very quickly, a matter of a few weeks, they drove Will and me to Nevada to get married, for they thought this was a good idea. He was a really good-looking guy, but I wasn't in love, nor was I prepared to jump in bed with a strange man. Scared to death, I froze up right off the very first night we were to sleep together.

Even though we had an apartment, we didn't live together as was intended, nor was the marriage consummated. Within three months, I got an annulment. During those few months, Will was so angry with me. He stole my small brand-new Falcon car I had just gotten from my grandparents and turned it into a hot rod. He ran with a bad crowd, and I never got my car back. This only proved to my grandparents and their friends that I truly was a bad person, a troublemaker, just like my mother. All through my formative years, they kept telling me I was going to be just like my mother. I vowed never to be like my mother, Terri, yet it seemed I was unknowingly duplicating her patterns of life.

Luciana, an Italian friend of my grandparents and Terri, helped me find a place to stay. She drove me over to the home of an elderly lady and dumped me there. All the while, this older lady, Fran, was refusing to take me in, not knowing anything about me. But Luciana ignored her and brought my suitcase and stuff into her home and departed. Reluctantly, Fran showed me to my bedroom and went back to her bed. I cried all night and a few nights after that.

After a few months to a year of having settled in, I left again, for I was not allowed to bring friends to her home and did not like her terrible dogs chewing up my clothes and shoes. She also wanted me to attend her Catholic church services with her, which I was not happy about at all since I had been forced by my grandparents to attend Masses, to no avail.

While living with Fran, my grandmother Noni and my sister Janie left for Italy to stay a few months, leaving my grandfather Nono behind to take care of himself. While the two of them were living it up and visiting relatives in Italy, Nono became very lonely and forlorn by himself.

One day, he knocked on Fran's door and asked to see me. I was surprised that he would come looking for me. He didn't look well, as though he had given himself too much insulin or not enough. He came in, but after just a few words to me, he turned around and departed, not really stating why he had come to see me. I felt sorry for him, but the thought to go check on him never came to my mind. I never visited him until Noni and Janie returned back home from Italy. Remorse crept in on me when I became a senior citizen for not visiting him and caring for him, but then as a young person, I didn't care to do so for the treatment I had received from them.

During the 1960s, my life went even more sour as those years passed. I was so happy to be out on my own, but was I really on my own? It proved not to be so free. Not having any life instructions, what's acceptable or not, left me very vulnerable. I wasn't completely stupid or in the dark, there just had been no good example in my life. There was just no good previous experience of being in the world alone. What's priority? What's not? What's acceptable, and what's not? How do I do this, or how do I do that? Life on the outside was frightening and unpredictable for me. I didn't know how to act or how to handle situations or what to say. I wondered what was normal.

My first job was with Pacific Tel. & Tel. at about 2.95 dollars an hour as a telephone operator. The job lasted a little over two years, frequently being promoted to various departments. But I wanted more of everything, so I quit. This started my job jumping every few months, trying to better myself.

One job landed me in a city hall as a clerk. The police department was in the next building. At times, they needed a relief phone person, and I would be sent over to assist.

One time, one of the higher-ranking officers came up behind me while I was taking an incoming call and slowly started pulling down my dress zipper on my back to about my waist then rubbing my back while I was still talking to the caller. I never reported him. How could I, for he was a lead police officer. I had started dating one of the police officers the week before. One of their detectives came to me and warned me to be very careful of him, for they suspected him of murdering his wife and said he kept his wife's belongings in the trunk of his car and that I happened to look just like her. Well, that ended that for me. I broke off any further contact with the suspect.

My job did not last long, for I had started frequenting various dance halls during the week to get my mind off the job and would wake up with a hangover the next morning from drinking and unable to perform my job very well at all. I never had trouble finding a job, just keeping it.

For three or four years in the mid-1960s, I continued going out drinking and dancing to big band music from the '20s and '30s four to five times during the week with Karen, a girlfriend I met at one of my many jobs. We thought it was the only way we could get our mind off the difficulties of life. We always got free drinks from guys, but our main goal was to dance and win the dance contests. We always dressed well and succeeded in finding the best dancers with our dance moves. All this time, it never dawned on me that I was following in my mother's and grandmother's footsteps. I would end up with a hangover almost every morning at work.

We never took anyone home or went to bed with any of them. Instead, we would go to the girl's room and ditch them. My girlfriend finally found a guy she liked and got married within a short time, ending our nights out. I was jealous about that and lonely. *What do I do now?* I kept thinking.

One time, late at night, I was followed home from the dance hall in a not-so-good business area to my cottage I was renting, and after arriving home, I could hear someone trying to break into my house. I called police, and two tall buffed-up young policemen came and looked around. Not finding anyone, they asked me if I would like for them to come and spend the night with me since they were about to get off duty. I politely said no and closed and locked the door and hoped they would not come back. They were more frightening than the noise I heard that caused me to call them in the first place.

From these dealings with policemen, I learned never to trust any of them, never suspecting there was an evil force, a family curse, to send me down the wrong path, enforcing negative actions in my life through lies of the devil. I usually believed whatever people in authority told me.

Having been denied new clothes in earlier years and through high school, I had an unquenchable thirst or drive for beautiful new clothes. I spent a great deal of my money on clothes. I was so impressed with Jackie Kennedy's manner of dress. I wanted to look just like her. I needed to feel good about myself, so I wore hats, white gloves, matching shoes and purse to match my dresses. It made me feel good, important, and lovely. The way I dressed or looked attracted many men. However, I was not successful in relationships or even staying on the jobs. Why does this sound familiar? Oh, yes, my mother's life was upon me, and I had no clue of it.

It became clear to me that I was not doing well in life, in relationships, in employment, or decent places to live I could afford.

One night, I decided to take my life. I wanted to die, to end the misery of life, but I didn't know how to do it. After driving around town late at night for a while, I gave up and stopped my car on the railroad tracks and waited and hoped for a train to come by and kill me. A bit of time went by, and then, out of the darkness, a car came up behind me and started honking for me to move. I tried to wave it by, but it just kept honking behind me. It made me so mad that I started the car and drove off. By this time, I had lost my nerve to try again. God's saving grace was at hand, unknown to me.

Eventually, I met a farm boy from Iowa through a coworker. We had drinks in a bar and danced, starting up a relationship ending in marriage. His name was Forrest, and a new adventure began for me. Our first few years were turbulent at times, for we did not spend much time to learn of each other. When he was drafted into the army, I moved back to my grandparents' house while I prepared to join him in Germany, where he was stationed. It was late 1967 by this time before I left to join Forrest in Germany. This adventure will be revealed in the next chapter.

One day, while I was staying with my grandmother during those two months, Noni was taking her heart medication, for she had developed heart trouble from a young age due to scarlet fever, according to the story she related to us in former years. Both Noni and Nono watched every penny they had. They were extremely conservative.

While she was preparing her coffee, she accidently dropped her open bottle of heart pills onto the counter. Several pills fell into her coffee cup and all over the counter and the floor. She picked up every last one and put them back into the bottle, but the ones that fell into her coffee dissolved. She was so stingy, she refused to throw the coffee away. Instead, she drank it, knowing the pills had fallen into it. She didn't want anything to go to waste.

The next morning, I could not awaken her from sleep. She had warned us often before that under no circumstance were we to take her to a hospital, for she was afraid she might die there, like Nono did a few months before. I called her Italian physician and told him the state she was in. He came immediately to the house and after examining her, called an ambulance.

He turned to me infuriated and asked why I didn't take action to call an ambulance. I relayed to him what she told me. He didn't believe me. Instead, he glared at me with an accusing, disrespectful look and said, "She could die, and you didn't do anything to help her." He was suggesting that my lack of action was on purpose to kill her.

I did not know how to reply. He apparently did not know how fearful I was to go against her wishes. My silence did not help the situation. She was taken to a local hospital, where I visited her later that day. Her face was one of torment and hell, as though she was visiting demons in hell. I had never seen that look before on anyone. I would not wish that despair on anyone. She died shortly after I left to go back to her home.

The doctor was right about my not calling an ambulance. I purposely did not call for an ambulance, for she said, "No, absolutely not," in conversations past. But for me to plan to kill her was not in me. As much as I disliked her for all the hell she put me through, it was not in my scope of reasoning. Many times I had prayed the Lord to take *me* home and spare *me* any more pain and suffering as she did to my mother. I did hate her for that. I would have continued under her cruel hand of discipline instead.

The doctor never took action against me. Nono had died three months before this, alone in a hospital. She never went to see him, and I was not told he was in a hospital until later, nor had I the thought to go see him. No one told me when he passed away, and I don't remember going to his funeral at all, nor do I remember going to Noni's funeral when she passed away, only wondering what was going to happen to all their treasures they held so dearly now that they were no longer present to hold on to it and preserve everything as they had done so well through the years. I didn't want much of anything of theirs. I just wanted to escape all of it. It was all left in the hands of the executor.

But store up for yourselves treasures in heaven, where neither moth nor rust destroys, and where thieves do not break in or steal; for where your treasure is there your heart will be also. (Matthew 6:20–21 NASB)

My tormentors now gone, I still didn't feel any relief from pressures of life. This is when I left everything behind and left for Germany to join Forrest, my husband, in the army, who was waiting for me. A new adventure was about to begin for me, and I was excited and anticipated a great new start in a better life, or so was *my* plan.

CHAPTER 6

Europe Adventure

Forrest was a sweet, fun-loving kid who grew up on the farm—you know, one of those kids who turned over outhouses while someone was inside doing their business. He drank beer pretty heavily, but I didn't think he had a problem with it until much later. A war, Vietnam, was going on in the '60s, and guys were getting drafted left and right. He didn't want to go. We talked about it and different ways of how he could get out of going. He decided to either move to Canada to avoid the draft or get married. He asked if I would marry him, and since my girlfriend Karen at the time got married and no one else was around to have fun with, I said yes.

We were not in love, and I am not sure either of us knew what love really was. Within two years of our marriage, he was drafted, to his total dismay. He was stuck in a marriage he really didn't want and still had to go to war. I refused his request for a divorce in the first year of marriage. Why? Because in the back of my head, I remembered my mother's many divorces. No, I didn't want to be like her—no divorce! Forrest was sent to Giessen, Germany, and within a year or so after my grandparents died, I followed him. During the second year of our marriage, before Giessen, I became pregnant, but something went wrong, and we lost the child, whom he wanted badly.

When I arrived, the first thing he asked for was money—all that I had. He had many bar bills to pay up and rent on a flat with a German family in Giessen he found for us to stay with. His drinking buddies visited us a lot, but I was determined to make things better for us. I planned a fourteen-day European tour bus trip from Frankfurt, Germany; through Austria; Switzerland; clear to Sicily, Italy; and back along the Mediterranean coast.

We started out in Frankfurt and proceeded to the Black Forest region of Germany. It was beautiful. Then we entered into Austria, and we found the culture different than that of Germany. For some reason, I thought all of Europe would be the same. Of course I took pictures throughout the trip. We went into Italy, visiting Venice and, of course, took a gondola ride, which was very romantic, except for the smell of sewage from the homes. I think Florence was my favorite city with all its finery and art. Milano came second. Rome was interesting and is where I bought the statue of Moses with horns.

Of course we visited the Vatican and actually went inside to take pictures of the pope as he passed by on a throne-like chair carried by several priests. I was not impressed; neither was Forrest. Statues in Italy were everywhere but we did not take note of what they represented. The Colosseum was extraordinary to look at. We made our way to Naples then Sicily, where we took a boat into the grottos, and visited graves in underground caves, viewing the petrified people and animals from volcanoes' lava flow in Pompeii centuries ago. I can't imagine the horror the people went through. Going back through Italy along the beautiful Mediterranean, we viewed the Ligurian Sea, visited the Tower of Pisa, Milano, and into Lucerne, Switzerland.

When we arrived back in Frankfurt, I was sad and not at all happy the trip was over, but Forrest was relieved and anxiously waiting to have a beer or two. It was our honeymoon that we never got. Of course, it was one of the better times in my entire life and his as well. Forrest couldn't drink as much on the trip, and I loved it. He was a loving and very gentle man when sober. We had seen countries we would not ordinarily have explored. It was fun, refreshing, and so educational, especially for this farm boy who had never been outside the US. The weather was colder than what we were used to, and we were not prepared for ice and snow in the Alps. I thought we would freeze to death with our lightweight summer clothes on.

It was so interesting and fun for me to take the bus or walk to the Giessen town center open market. A wife of one of Forrest's buddies became friends with me, and we would bundle up warmly and walk to town or take the bus to explore the various foods and items for sale to locals, many tourists, and army people stationed there. We fell in love with the breads and veggies, which were different than those at home in the United States. The weather always seemed colder than what we were used to…lots of snow. So much to see and the temptation to buy was heavy. Unfortunately, we had little cash to splurge on desirable treasures or souvenirs.

A very humorous thing happened the first week I arrived there. I had bought a fancy black negligee to wear for Forrest's sake with a matching robe to go with it. When I went into the kitchen, which we shared with the German family, to get something to drink with my negligee and robe on, the family saw me, and they were amazed at how beautiful I looked (or so they thought) and asked where I was going out for such a grand celebration. When I told them I was going to bed and this was my nightgown, they were flabbergasted that I wore such an elaborate outfit to bed. I learned later the men and women there wear long heavy cotton, flannel-like nightshirts to be warm. It became a standing joke. They thought we were extremely extravagant. They were a poor family sharing their home with military people to meet their financial needs. They would ask us to buy food at the commissary for them, and I often did.

Prior to our stay in Germany, we tried to have children, as I mentioned before, and after those years of trying, I had a miscarriage—hemorrhaged in my third or fourth month—and was taken to a local base hospital while still in the US. Doctors said they were going to do a D&C on me. I had no idea what that meant, nor did they explain it to me, and I was in too much pain to ask or hold a conversation. I just simply agreed to get rid of the pain. But it also got rid of the baby boy I was carrying. I never felt like a mother or planned for the baby's birth. It seemed more like an illness to me. Forrest was so devastated and couldn't understand why we lost the child. Neither could I. Now, in my seventies, I realize I was still under the generational curse from previous generations and specifically, my grandmother. At that time, I had no idea or understanding of spiritual matters.

My mother's abortion was a boy before she bore me. I was following in the same footsteps as predicted by my grandparents, who constantly spoke out curses over me. I just aborted a boy child! Strange how I never grieved over the loss of the child. It was as though I was never pregnant. I never read the Word of God and had no knowledge of these things, spiritual things. We were both so blind.

So army time was ending in Germany, and I was finally able to conceive a child while there. We were extremely elated and proud. I kept pushing my stomach out as much as I could to show everyone I was pregnant. We flew back to California to our home, which we had bought from Nono. Nono had bought a very small home for my sister Janie, who had gotten married, but they refused it for whatever reason. We had taken over the house and had it rented out while in Germany.

I was able to carry the baby a little over eight months, but one day, we were visiting Forrest's brother out of town across from an airport, and while we were there, I became terrified of the airplanes flying so low over the home because of extremely loud noise. I thought they were landing on top of us and became so frightened that my water broke, to my dismay. I was rushed to the doctor's office, and the doctor told me there was a problem. The child was born breech and premature. We had a baby girl, whom we named Elizabeth. We were so happy. We now have a baby, our baby!

Forrest was drinking heavier than ever now. At times, I would find him white or gray in color and stone-cold on the floor. So stiff was he, I couldn't bend his arms, and I took him for being dead. I did not want this lifestyle for my daughter or myself. I wanted her to have a much better life than I ever had. We both had similar dreams of the lifestyle we wanted together, but we were not able to obtain it due to his alcoholism and my inability to cope or understand. We were very depressed people much of the time, so I started contemplating what I should do about this situation since Forrest refused to get counseling with me. He felt there was nothing wrong with our marriage, that I was just being unreasonable.

Within six months of Elizabeth's birth, the doctors discovered for sure that she was crippled in her hips and said she would not be able to walk without surgery. Forrest was extremely depressed over this and refused any treatment for her, saying it was not necessary. Pride got in the way of rational thinking. This couldn't happen to him was his thinking.

By this time, we had moved into a more expensive house on a hillside in Belmont, California. Forrest had torn out the back door and part of the back wall, saying he was remodeling the place. I decided to file for a divorce. I had had enough! He refused to get sober, saying he was not an alcoholic; he just liked his beer. "What's wrong with that?"

Elizabeth was having trouble crawling and was not walking. I found an apartment and moved out with Elizabeth, leaving the house to Forrest with no alimony or child support coming into us. I soon learned that was a big mistake! Immediately, my mind was on getting medical help for Elizabeth. A very famous, world-renowned physician at Stanford Hospital did surgery to try to repair her hips by putting steel bars in her hip and then a body cast from her chest to her toes for two months to allow bones to grow and form, but it didn't work. She had physical therapy after that, but it was unsuccessful. She was able to eventually walk but with difficulty and pain.

The divorce went through, and Elizabeth and I began a new life again—with much turmoil, I might add. I worked a full-time job plus two part-time jobs in evenings, never getting ahead. Elizabeth spent lots of time with babysitters. At one point, when I went to get her, she didn't want to come home with me and was calling her sitter *Mommy*. The couple had been conditioning her to stay with them without my knowledge.

It killed my spirit, and I had to make a decision. Do I go on working and find a lot of different sitters, or do I just sign up for welfare and stay home with her? I was not raised to depend on government handouts. I decided going on welfare would be a very bad example for her. Depending on handouts just didn't cut it for me, so I continued working hard and employing various babysitters. Elizabeth got bounced around a lot from sitter to sitter, most of whom had injured her in one way or another.

I hated my life. I hated being single and alone. I desired that beautiful, perfect marriage you read about in books or you see in the movies and hear about. I could only dream of it "in want."

Surely my marriage to Forrest could have worked out with help if we had only known to seek out the Lord. We didn't seek out Christian or secular help because we just didn't think to do that, and we both hated the way we were forced into religion growing up. We never attended any church. We believed the lies handed down to us from generation to generation.

Forrest was the youngest of many siblings from a broken and dysfunctional home. His parents were not divorced but extremely religious to a fault. To find some sort of comfort in life and numb the hurt he was enduring, he took to drinking like some of his older siblings. It didn't work for him; he was dysfunctional. My family was steeped in mysterious ways and secrets. They had various superstitions, witchcraft, prejudice, and more handed down from their forefathers, which they never questioned.

We were a very dysfunctional family even though we went to confession and Mass once a month. Neither of us knew any other way of life or how to change. We both hated our life. We were stuck in a rut.

Forrest was a loving, kind, hardworking, compassionate person. He wanted to make something of himself and get ahead in life. Unfortunately, he was unable to see his addiction, which hindered his employment, and I was so opposed to heavy drinking after seeing what alcohol did in my own family. I was tired of it and didn't want that for Elizabeth either. I had given up any hope for us, for the marriage. Forrest was deceived as I was and believed the lies the adversary delivered to him and me.

So thankful am I that Forrest and I were together in Germany for two years and that we had that excitement and joy traveling and exploring Europe. Those are beautiful memories in a very bleak time of war and change in our country of America and in us. That was the closest relationship I ever had with anyone. So now I was left alone in life again.

Forrest suffered a premature death in 1984 at the age of forty-two due to melanoma. He had three cancerous tumors in his brain, which caused severe pain and aggression. When he discovered he had cancer, he sought the Lord for help by attending a Catholic church with his then-new wife Janet, and Elizabeth. I can only pray he was able to receive the Lord in his heart.

Now, looking back, I believe we could have had a good, successful marriage if we had sought the Lord and there was good, godly counseling available. Yet I realize we had a mindset that wouldn't have allowed the Lord in our lives at that time. How tragic since we were both brought up in so-called religious homes. Neither of us was saved or even knew what it meant to be saved.

> The Lord looks down from heaven on all mankind to see if there are any who understand, and who seek God. All have turned away; all have become corrupt; there is no one who does good, not even one. (Psalm 14:2–3 NASB)

Spiritual transformation

To be truly free, you have to break free, let loose of a lifetime of the old dead ways of doing things. There has to be a transformation in your mind that takes place to move you into a spiritual position and operate from that spiritual level. The enemy is going to try and come against you with anything and everything he can to keep you from a stronger level of faith. He, the enemy, does not want you to learn how to speak with power and authority to move mountains (your burdens).

Instead of speaking the problem, we must speak with authority in Christ to the burden with His promises. Life and death are truly in the power of your tongue, and God wants you to speak life. We must change our thinking from carnal to a spiritual mindset, which is healing to our bones. Negative words spoken out bring defeat. Spiritual words build us up, edifies us, and brings greater faith, hope, joy, peace, and tranquility.

It is never too late to look for change, to be the person you were created to be. We are each a valuable and unique person, a treasure to God.

CHAPTER 7

Living in Deception

Many times I would come home to my residence(s), and I would have a strange feeling that someone might have broken in and was hiding, waiting for me. One time, a man I had dated after my divorce from Forrest was hiding in my bedroom closet and did jump out and hit me, yelling something at me when I opened the closet door, then ran out the front door. I don't remember the circumstance that caused this invasion and beating or what he said. I also remember looking under my bed and behind doors a lot as well as behind shower curtains. The memory of my mother's episodes came back to haunt me.

One of the more memorable times that stand out in my mind is when Elizabeth was a toddler. I was dating an older man, Mitch, about ten years my senior with a vintage two-seater T-Bird. He was soft spoken and seemed to be a mild-mannered man who smoked a pipe with a brocaded smoking jacket on at his house. I was taken by his manner and looks, or perhaps it was my need for a father figure, and it seemed he might fit the bill.

Elizabeth and I were invited to his apartment for dinner. I had fixed a really nice dinner, and Mitch made spaghetti as well. While we were eating, Elizabeth didn't like something one of us had made, and she wouldn't eat it, so he got up angrily from his chair, yelling at her to eat it, and started taking off his belt to whip her. Not believing this could happen, I jumped up and said I had to go to the bathroom. I ran into the other room and could hear Elizabeth crying, saying, "No, no."

I froze. I was unable to move. Fear for my life and scenes of my mother's brutal beatings came to mind. I could not rescue or save Elizabeth. She got whipped, and I was powerless to do anything, frozen in time. I don't have any memory how that evening ended, but I'm sure it was awful for both of us.

It brought back a memory of how Fester, my mother's last husband, did the same thing to me when I was around six to eight years old. I did not like pearl onions from a jar they opened up and refused to eat one. Fester took off his belt and beat me until I ate some. Then he got mad because I needed to regurgitate. My mother did nothing that I can remember. She was frozen, paralyzed in fear, I suppose, remembering how she also disappeared came to my mind. Somehow I continued seeing this man on and off, for he loved fishing as I did, and we went fishing together a few times along with Elizabeth. As I later discovered, he had been married six or more times and had children all over the United States that he was paying child support to, and he was still married to the last woman he married.

Somehow, in my confused and needy state of mind, I continued seeing him, and he invited me to go to Las Vegas for a weekend with him, so I made arrangements to leave Elizabeth behind with a sitter. When we arrived in Las Vegas and had gotten a room, he simply dismissed me and said he wanted to go his own way for the day, and I should do the same. *What?* I thought to myself. *He's dumping me here.*

After wandering around the gamblers all day and playing some of the slot machines, I met a young businessman who took an interest in me and gave me money to play games along with him, eventually leading up to inviting me to his hotel room. By this time, he was so drunk, he threw a hundred-dollar bill at me and passed out on the bed even though we did not have any physical contact. I was humiliated that he threw money at me as though I was a prostitute, but I decided since Mitch dumped me, I might need the money for a bus ticket back home, and I grabbed it and quickly left for the room Mitch secured for the two of us to stay.

Mitch was there waiting for me and was infuriated and started cursing and yelling at me, telling me how disgusting and rotten women are, not worth toilet paper and horrible detestable things. His words were like a knife in my heart, and I felt my life was just not worth living. I would never be able to do anything right.

When we finally got back to my apartment the next day, I was so despondent, I took an entire bottle of Prozac, swallowing every one of the pills. For whatever reason, I then ran outside to his car as he was leaving to tell him what I did in hopes of punishing him, but he took hold of me and pushed me back to the apartment and raped me then left me for dead on my bed.

Two days later, I woke up disappointed that I was still alive yet relieved and bewildered. I was alive! It seemed dying just wasn't measured out for me. "Why, Lord?" I kept asking. I had to figure out what day it was and get myself together. It came to me that I have a child, Elizabeth. "Oh, my God, what have I done?

By the time I got to the sitter's home, they were livid with me and boldly said they would like to adopt Elizabeth from me and would take very good care of her. Another knife was just plunged into my heart. I felt very guilty and unworthy. After telling them I didn't need their services any longer, I took Elizabeth away, quickly kissing her cheeks and hugging her all the way home. She's mine, and I need her. I could not bear to lose her. I remained confused about life as time continued on.

This was about the time I purchased a small wooden mahogany boat with a small engine to take up fishing in the Delta. I love the water and the taste of most fish, so I thought this would be a great outdoor sport for Elizabeth and me to do together. She loved it—the water, boating, and the fishing.

After several months, I decided we needed a larger boat that we could sleep in overnight at the Delta and purchased a turquoise fiberglass boat with seats that made into beds and a cloth cover like you would find on a convertible car. It held twenty gallons of gas and was much more suitable for fishing. Elizabeth and I loved exploring the

Delta, and I spent many weekend nights on board—not so many fish caught, however. My boating eventually came to a tragic end when I became involved with a man called Drake, who sold it out from under me without my consent rather than making minor repairs as I requested.

After other similar encounters with men and women throughout the 1970s, I started searching for help by checking out various denominational churches. Since I thought Elizabeth was a miracle from God, I thought I might find *Him, God*, in a church somewhere. I settled for a while in a Baptist church, which I later found turned out to be very liberal, that was in a neighboring town. There, I began reading the Bible a little and making friends. They needed someone to teach children ages six to twelve, so I volunteered. They gave me a preplanned monthly program, and I started in. It was invigorating to learning as I was teaching, but I still had no idea yet what it meant to be saved. I was having a lot of fun teaching the kids and preparing for the classes. Can you imagine teaching a subject you know nothing about?

Trying to date mostly outside the church was not working very well. I had put an ad in the personal section of the local newspaper looking for a mate. The creeps who came to my door were almost unbelievable. One in particular was a tall black-haired man with black eyes dressed in all black with black shades who knocked on my door. When I answered the knock, he stuck his foot in the door threshold so I could not close the door. So I invited him in all the way. He said looking straight at me, "Do you realize I could murder you?"

My mind just did not want to process that thought, and I said, "No."

Without much further conversation, he took me to a Greek restaurant, food I didn't care for, and we hardly spoke a word to each other. I was returned home quickly after the meal, and I never heard from him again. You ask why I would go out with him in the first place. I can only presume it was out of fear and not knowing what to do, how to handle myself in various situations. Little did I know that I kept drawing attention from unstable people, mostly men. Victims or troubled people, as I was, attract the same kind of people: victims, abusers, and troubled people.

Having found a position with a semiconductor company in accounting, I was elated, but in the first two days of my employment, my immediate supervisor, Ted, informed me that if I intended to keep my job or get promoted, I would have to put out. What? Is he really saying what I think he is saying? I did not respond at all. By the end of the week, Ted said he wanted to come to my apartment to visit and get better acquainted. I said, "Sure," not believing he would really come, but he did with a bottle of wine in hand.

No sooner than he came inside the living room he started to pull down his pant zipper, all the while looking around for a place to have sex with me. Panic struck me, and I told him I forgot he was coming and that I was not feeling well at all; probably the flu or very bad cold was overtaking me. He left promptly but was visually disappointed.

The next business day, I told his boss about the encounter, only to learn his boss was having an affair with a coworker himself even though he was married with children. He didn't think anything was amiss with Ted's visitation to my house. Where was the integrity? There were other men in various departments also having affairs and did not try to hide it. The company folded after a few months of my working there. Can you wonder why?

As I sit here (now year 2019) and recount all these things, I praise God he has taken away that fear, the bondage I was in, and that He has sustained Elizabeth and me with His grace and mercy. Even though I did not yet know Him or receive Him, He was there all the time. I had not yet come to that realization of God in my life at that time. How grateful and wonderful it is that now I can hear His voice inside of me, telling me how much He loves me just as I am and have forgiven me of my past wrongs. I could not hear His voice back then, nor did I really know Him.

As I mentioned earlier, I was divorced from Forrest in the 1970s, with Elizabeth age three then, and I started going to this Baptist church, where I started teaching children's church. As I was teaching ages six through twelve, Drake, a six-foot-six-inch person, was working with older kids and assisting one of the pastors/counselors. I certainly was not attracted to him due to his long unkempt hair and long scraggly beard and scruffy clothes.

One Sunday after Thanksgiving, he came to church with a very short well-trimmed beard and short haircut—quite an improvement. He actually looked respectable, and I spoke to him for the first time by complimenting him on his *hairdo* and trimmed beard. He explained he had gone back to see his parents and siblings in Arkansas for the Thanksgiving holiday. While he was there, his relatives took scissors to his hair and beard, he claimed. He actually looked presentable.

Elizabeth and I had gone to someone's Thanksgiving dinner that year, but I loved cooking and had fixed a turkey and other dishes for her and me to celebrate at home. Elizabeth was flirting with him, and he was being, well, nice to her, so I decided to ask half-heartedly if he was doing anything for dinner.

Being a Good Samaritan, as I thought I was at that moment, I decided it would be nice to have a less-fortunate, downcast person over to enjoy a decent meal and some company. That was a huge—giant—mistake. He came and played with Elizabeth when we were not eating or conversing, and she was having a good time. I was relieved when he finally left, though—he definitely was not my type of person—but at least he attended church and was active in it. At that time, I thought that was a really big deal. I had been having a lot of blind dates—all failures, and some were dangerous characters.

None of the men I dated wanted anything to do with church or religion, except one neurotic short older guy. He was Italian, had a high-paying work position, and was looking for a Catholic wife who would stay home and give him lots of children—at least ten, he said—and cook big meals for his friends and family. After a few dates, he was immediately talking marriage. In every conversation we had, he would bring up his mother and what kind of wife she wanted for him and expected—*big turn off!* Remembering doctors told me I could not have any children—and per chance if I did, they would be severely disabled—I could see it now! Furthermore, every time we drove by a Catholic church, he would make the sign of the cross on himself and say some prayer in Italian, a religion I had no intentions of revisiting.

Since Drake and I attended the same church, it was hard to avoid him. Anyway, he did seem to have a girlfriend of sorts in that church. I couldn't quite put my finger on it. Later, I discovered they had intimate relations now and then. She seemed to be a happy, backwoods type of woman with long hair who did not believe in shaving. They would make a good team if he kept his long hair and long beard, kind of like the backwoods Alaskan people in documentaries on TV I had viewed once.

Well, it somehow came about that we started dating, not at first but after we both attended Pastor Fox's sexuality class at this Baptist church. Yep! One day, Pastor Fox approached me in the church hallway and looked straight into my face and eyes and said, "You need this sexuality class!"

I did not know what his sexuality class really was. I took it as a blatant accusation that I had a problem with my sexuality and it needed fixing. So wanting to be a better person, I signed up, still not knowing what I was getting into.

Drake asked me if I was going, and I reluctantly said yes. He said he was going and asked, "Why don't we go together?" I agreed to do so as not to be alone.

Many people were involved—twenty-five to thirty—mostly couples. Drake's girlfriend, the one with the long hair, came and did not know Drake and I came together. It surprised her. I wonder if this was Drake's way of telling her their affair was over, or was it?

To my surprise and dismay, Pastor Fox started talking about how *sex* was God's gift to man and should be enjoyed to the fullest, whether you were married or not! He showed movie clips of unmarried couples, adults, and youth having sex in various positions in bed and in a swimming pool. He had question and answer sessions throughout the two-day seminar. The first night, he told everyone to go home and experiment with each other and have fun because God made sex for us to enjoy. It was a gift; take it. The class made me nervous and anxious, seeing and discussing naked people enjoying sex. This was a totally forbidden area for me growing up, as I was told it was evil, and did not want to have intimate relations without being married to the man of my dreams, which I had yet to figure out what that was.

Of course, since I had driven Drake there, I had to take him home to his apartment. He invited me up to his apartment, expecting me to say yes, but failed to tell me he was sharing it with someone. Out of curiosity, I went. The apartment smelled awful, like a dirty gym locker room. There were dirty dishes lying around everywhere, along with what seemed like dirty clothes thrown here and there.

He said his roommate was gay! That was another shock. Why was he living with a gay man?

When I questioned him about it, he said, "I just wanted to experience how gay people live," and very quickly directed me to the one and only bedroom and bed that appeared to not have been made or changed in weeks.

My heart said, *Turn around and run for your life*, but instead, I was led around as though I had a ring on my nose, and he was pulling me on it. The fear in me of his being so big and strong, not knowing what he might do to me if I turned and ran, I just gave in to receive the consequences of giving in to him. It is very difficult to remember how I was seduced by him on our very first encounter. Shame and disgust came over me and a great dislike for myself. I felt like a frozen object and just wanted the visit to be over and to get out of that place. This free gift of sex from God was disgusting, yet I ended up staying that night, feeling obligated and afraid to leave for fear of what he may do to me even though it was not enjoyable to say the least. I felt dirty and that no amount of hot showers would make me feel clean. I felt I was just not a good person.

The next morning, we had to go back to the sexuality class. Instead of taking the elevator down, he led me through an outside stair door. I had a lot of fear then, and when I saw that I was on a see-through metal staircase four stories up, I froze, became paralyzed, and could not take one step in any direction. I knew I was going to die falling to the ground.

This made him extremely angry. Instead of trying to calm me down and talk me through it, he cursed and could not understand why I was so fearful of falling and shamed me down the stairs. He refused to go back in and take the elevator down, saying, "The door locked automatically when it closed behind us."

I was even more humiliated and shamed by the time we got to the church to continue the sex class. The images I saw in that class stayed with me for most of my life. I didn't know how to deal with the embarrassment and humiliation that had taken place.

Pastor Fox invited me to his home for further counseling, seeing as how he thought I was in such need of it. While I was there, he suffered great pain in his body and had to stop his counseling. So deeply engaged was I in that Baptist church, teaching Sunday school to kids six to twelve years of age out of their promoted books on sexuality for children, which included masturbating as a way for kids to control their sex drive.

Elizabeth was in my class up until December 1981. I remember, in horror now, Matthew 18:6: "but whoever causes one of these little ones who believe in Me to stumble it would be better for him to have a heavy millstone hung around his neck, and to be drowned in the depth of the sea." Even though I asked the Lord for forgiveness and went through many sessions of forgiving myself, it left a scar on my heart. Obviously, this was not your typical Baptist church. This one was steeped in deception and evil.

God is able to intervene and release us from bondages and troubles that shackle us. Through faith in Jesus (Yeshua in Hebrew), we can all be set free and healed if we call on Him with all our heart. Why didn't I call on Him?

After the episode with Drake and the sexuality class, I felt stuck, for most of the congregation knew what the class was about and who attended. I felt as long as I was on staff as an elder and bookkeeper at that church and was learning the Bible, I had better make the best of it. I was worried about losing custody of Elizabeth or rumors that I was sleeping around. Elizabeth was attracted to Drake, and I decided to do what the pastor suggested: "Try him out." We lived together for two years before we married in winter of 1975 for me to keep custody of Elizabeth.

Elizabeth's father Forrest and his wife Janet were making threatening phone calls to me, saying I was prostituting and an unfit mother. They were going to take custody of her. I made Drake aware of what was being said by them. Drake's marriage proposal was not one for the record books and right on the heels of the child support dispute. Drake was contemplating over something and turned and said, "I can't find any reason to not marry you, so I guess we could get married. What do you think?"

Already knowing I was stuck between a rock and a hard place no matter whether we broke up or I married him, the outcome was not what I wanted. I only knew I could not lose Elizabeth. I answered and said, "Yeah, I guess." There was no love for Drake, but I thought it was the best solution to make sure Elizabeth was not taken from me. I believed the lies that were spoken by everyone. I had a desperate need. I couldn't lose Elizabeth like I lost my mother Terri and my half brother Joseph. My thought was I could learn to love Drake if I tried hard enough.

The Lord knew I was searching for Him, for He never left or abandoned me when I fell deeper into sin. The church decided to have a talent contest and signed various people up to perform for the rest of congregants and the public (as an outreach). Three of us, ladies, signed up to be belly dancers. I had been taking belly dancing classes and made my own outfit for classes. Being the oldest, I should have known it was not of God. Receiving that kind of gross attention didn't go well with me. I believe I knew it was wrong but as usual, went along with everyone. After all, aren't these church people?

I could see eyes of contempt and lust staring at me in the audience while I danced. Drake signed up as a magician and made his own costume to prove he could sew as well as I could or better to compete with me as usual.

Drake had been smoking and hiding marijuana at various places in my house without my knowledge through the years and actually growing some while telling me they were a type of tomato plant, which never seemed to bear fruit. He even had some hidden in the attic. After trying marijuana out with him, I decided I hated it, for it rendered me powerless over my actions, which was extremely important to me to have control of myself.

One day, I had to call the police department to report six hundred dollars in cash I had on my dining room table was stolen, disappeared. A detective came, not a cop, and looked all over the house. Not finding anything, he left and told me never to leave cash lying around in the house. Drake was present and nervous and had a guilty face and seemed worried, but I had no idea of what. Now, years later, I realize had the detective found the marijuana Drake stashed in the attic without my knowledge, we could have been arrested, and Elizabeth would have been taken away, and I realize Drake had taken the money for himself, although he did not admit it, and was furious that I had called the police. Why wouldn't I have called? It was my hard-earned money that was missing. My home was supposed to be a safe place.

Now when I look back at my life with Drake, I am astonished that the Lord protected Elizabeth and me as He did. It could have been much worse. CPS could have come in and removed Elizabeth from me several times. Drake and I could have been arrested for possession. So many horrible things could have happened, but they didn't, except for Elizabeth's and my abuse. I did not know God was right there all the time. All I had to do was call out to *Him* and believe, seek His face with all my heart. I was so broken. I felt I was just not worthy or good enough for Him to help me.

Remembering when I was ten years old and entered a drawing contest, I got a reply back by mail stating my artwork was very good and could have won, except that I was too young to be in the contest. My desire to draw and paint stayed with me through the years. After Elizabeth was born and we were living with Drake, I took up painting classes at a local college and loved it so much. I stayed with it for about one year, then continued painting on my own at home. I brought some of my paintings to my place of employment and sold every one of them. There were several commissioned paintings of people and their favorite pet. One place I worked had barrels of discarded semiconductor chips, which I was able to take home and turn into high-rise city silhouettes on painted canvas using glue and a quirky imagination. People loved them. They all got sold for a good price.

When Elizabeth was around nine or ten years of age, I had her photo taken at a studio and later decided to paint her picture in oils. I still have that painting to this day hanging in my living room. That was an extremely bad time in her life, so she doesn't care to look at it, reminding her of the hardships she had to endure. To this day, I still paint when my arms and hands are not numb and in pain from the damage to my spine through the years. I praise God for all He has shown me and given me the ability to do. He gives each one of us special gifts to use here on earth. How awesome is the God of all creation!

During the first seven years of my marriage to Drake, in the house I had purchased, I decided to raise rabbits for food and pelts, hoping to make some extra money in the process. I had four females and one buck and bred them according to instructions and info I researched on rabbit breeding. The meat was better tasting and easier to digest than chicken. Unknowingly, I slaughtered them in the Kosher way, hanging them by their feet so all the blood would drain out of the meat, which I knew nothing about then. It just seemed logical.

I saved all the pelts and tried to cure them myself, unsuccessfully I might add. So I sent them off to a tannery for processing and a few years later, made two large rabbit blankets with the pelts. One of blankets sold for two hundred dollars. They were beautiful. I never did make money with the rabbits, except for an occasional sale of a dressed rabbit. The manure was excellent for the vegetable garden I had. When it was slaughtering time, Elizabeth freaked out due to their childlike screams if I didn't knock them out on the head hard enough. It would send her running into the house to hide and get away from the pitiful screams they would make.

There was so much deception and irresponsibility during our marriage. One occurrence was when Elizabeth was molested by the babysitter's thirty-year-old son. Elizabeth didn't tell me. I found out from her father during a very angry phone call from him, after which I reported it to the cops at the police station. Days after the report

Drake apparently intercepted a court order for Elizabeth to appear in court to testify against the perpetrator, for he told me he was taking Elizabeth to the courthouse for a hearing, leaving me standing stupidly as they walked out the front door with a grin on his face. I had no idea there was a court date!

According to Elizabeth's recount decades later, Drake dropped her off outside the courthouse and never went in with her. Elizabeth was only nine years old at the time. Surely, the judge asked where her parents were. Why would a judge or even a police officer allow her to testify or leave without a parent or even an adult with her? The question I had for myself was, why did I not drop everything I was doing and follow them to the courthouse? I have no answer.

I suspect Drake had an ulterior motive for not telling me or letting me go with them to the courthouse, for he always favored men and would justify their actions over women. I was never told of the outcome even though I asked. It was as though it was none of my business to them. Children's Social Services could have and rightly should have taken Elizabeth from me for neglect. *Why didn't they?* Even though I was not there for her, God was watching out for us is my only explanation.

Drake was openly seeing two women where he was employed and told me he was going scuba diving with one of them. He said I could come along, and I did as I had taken up diving also. However, they left me alone under the water while they went exploring other areas. Here we are, professing to be Christians working in the church, even on staff and leading others. What's wrong with this picture?

Obviously, I knew Drake was playing around with other women while we were married, but I was determined not to get a divorce at the first, second, third, or more signs of trouble. I did not want to get married and divorced multiple times "like my mother." So with that mindset, I stuck it out…until one day when Elizabeth came to me and said she was afraid of Drake…that he might do something to her!

Seeing her face and the fear, it hit me like a ton of bricks. *Oh, my god! Now I have a possible sexual problem with him assaulting my daughter! No! That is not going to happen!* I took an immediate about-face. Instead of going to court to keep custody of her and not let her father and his wife get custody, which they were in the process of doing the second time around, I called my attorney to drop my case without any explanation. I did not want anyone to know I was married to a possible pedophile person or worse. I did not give Drake an explanation for my action, leaving him bewildered and wondering, but he never pursued the issue with me.

Now December 1981, I quickly called her father and asked if he would take her and raise her without any explanation to him or Elizabeth. I knew he would not harm her, for he loved her dearly. I failed to protect my only child. How blind can a parent be? Now I have lost her and may never get her back. Of course, they came immediately and took her, leaving many of her belongings behind. I did not say anything to them or to anyone else of my suspicions regarding Drake. It never dawned on me that Elizabeth might think I didn't want her anymore and was giving her away. I just could not tell her the truth out of fear of consequences to us both.

My intimate and day-to-day relationship with Drake was not normal or right. I didn't really know what was *right* due to false teachings from the church and no teaching at home growing up in such a dysfunctional family. The pastors I sought counsel with on the matter, mostly men, did not believe me and tried to discredit my testimony even when I reported rapes. It was my "duty as a wife to be supportive of my husband," they would say, "for he is the head of the family, and you must obey him." Again, this is not your usual Baptist-church response. They refused to see the abuse and wrongs done to me, so it seemed there was only one solution: divorce.

Sometime during the first two years I lived with Drake, he told me he had been practicing ESP (extrasensory perception) and transcendental meditation and found it gave him peace and gratification. Not knowing what that was, I asked for an explanation. "What is that?" He said he was able to sit with another person and mentally/spiritually go into that person in front of him and that he could spiritually travel to another location or to another person. He asked if I wanted to meditate with him. I didn't like the whole idea of leaving my body to go anywhere, except maybe heaven, and I sure didn't want anyone trying to get into my body, spirit, or soul. I turned him down, but he continued to practice projection alone or with someone else. In my mind, I felt it was evil and scary.

Years later after our divorce when I was living in Bent Oak, Oklahoma, I felt his tangible spirit present in my home. It gave me chills up and down my spine. It was eerie and felt evil. I had no training on how to dispel that sort of thing, so I just simply told the spirit to *go*. Eventually, he—it—did leave. This event brought to mind the evil my mother and grandparents participated in when I was a toddler. I hated it.

Now I recognize why our home was filled with evil spirits and why Elizabeth's packed-up toys in the closet would start playing without being touched when I was alone in the house. My dogs would bark and growl at something invisible in the corner of a room, which made me believe there was an evil spirit lurking around. Strangely, no one detected these spirits when we had Bible study in our home. Pastors and congregants never discussed or brought to light that things like this could happen and what should be done about it. Apparently, no one discerned the evil, or they were afraid to disclose it and deal with it.

Where was God in all this? I wondered many times. Mind you, I was a faithful attendee every Sunday, hoping to hear *His* voice concerning my life. At times I begged God to take me home—*I quit!* Other times, I felt I could start all over again but had the attitude of being a useless, no-good, sinful, terrible, shameful human being whom no one really liked or wanted. I felt I was damaged goods. Yet God was there transforming or remolding me quietly unbeknownst to me. I thought He was making me suffer for being such a terrible person.

Looking back, I found we had trouble or difficulty in apologizing, to admit we were wrong, and unable to take responsibility for wrongs we did to each other or others we dealt with. We were suffering from a hard heart, a heart filled with pride, selfishness, unwillingness to repent of our wrongs, which were sins not allowing us to forgive and change. This is what wrecks people's lives; breaks up families; destroys marriages; even splits congregations, which I have seen more than once; and initiates violence and destruction. This is not what any loving person would want. It's not what I wanted or anyone would want, but that's what we get—a hard heart—when we refuse to repent of *our* ways or even try to see *our* error.

Neither of us was able to admit we were wrong or even see the sin. Our spiritual eyes were closed to some degree concerning ourselves. We could see the log—the sin—in everyone else's eye, not ours. Either we were very good actors, acting out our lives through lies, or the church failed miserably to see our folly and make any attempts to correct us. Who's to blame? We, the perpetrators, are guilty. We listened and believed the lies of the devil and in turn, teach the very same to others.

Within the Baptist church we attended, Halloween was a huge deal, a big scary celebration, and Drake and I, along with other congregants, went all out to try and scare the life out of the kids and adults. Drake was interested in keeping up with daily horoscopes and his sign. I recall a company party we went to where we had our palms read by a palm reader in the first seven years of our marriage. It's no wonder I was always wrestling with him and the spirits. I recall being tired and lying down on my sofa and feeling demons jumping on me and my going down (spiraling down) a deep dark hole. The only thing that saved me was finding enough air/breath to speak the word *Jesus*, and the spirits got off me and left. It made me feel mentally and physically ill and afraid to be alone in the house. Who could I tell of these happenings?

They actually baptized people in this congregation…of which I was a participant. For some reason, it was an extremely emotional occurrence in my life, for I could not stop crying, and I could not explain to anyone why I was crying, which disturbed Drake and the senior pastor, who was doing the baptizing. It changed me somehow, but I could not say just how, except that I felt like a better person for a while.

A few weeks to a couple of months after Elizabeth was sent to her father to live—I just can't remember exact dates—I had become so despondent with her gone and with what was happening between Drake and me, problems at work and at church, and tormenting memories I contemplated over my life, whether I should just give up and kill myself to get rid of the pain. I reasoned that I would never see Elizabeth again, and I was in a marriage I never wanted in the first place. I went to the kitchen drawer and found an ice pick I thought might work…if I could just plunge it into my heart. I crouched down to the floor against the kitchen cabinets and put the ice pick to my heart, anticipating soon it would be my last breath, and the suffering would be over.

Just as I was ready to proceed Drake came through the kitchen door from the garage and saw what I was doing. He stopped and looked at me intently then put a huge smile on his face and started giggling and walked out of the room into the hall as though it didn't matter. In that second, I heard a still, small voice inside of me, telling me to go see Numan. He was a relative of Drake's living in Hawaii. I got up and put away the ice pick and got my phone to call him and made arrangements to fly there. Now I realize this was God hiding His face and acting from behind the scene.

When I came back from the great miracle and awakening in Hawaii in 1982, we were still attending the liberal Baptist church. Dreams and visions within me took place, and I had a very disturbing dream of the church roof collapsing during an earthquake, falling on all the congregants, killing most everyone, even though I ran into the church yelling for everyone to get out quickly, warning them of the impending doom. No one paid attention.

I related the dream to Drake, but he did not believe, nor did the pastor when I related it to him. The senior pastor said I probably had too much pizza before bedtime. I felt it was a warning to the pastors to stop the evil teachings going forth, or this would be the consequences. Pastor Fox was then experiencing severe pain in his body, rendering him unable to walk. To this day, I believe Pastor Fox believed and taught the lies of the enemy, Satan.

Three days after the dream, a church in Los Angeles was overcome by the roof caving in on them, injuring many and killing some. Drake and the pastor then thought that was possibly what my dream was about and dismissed it. It seemed that men were always right and women were discredited in this church. I truly believe the dream was a warning to the leaders of this church and to me because of the evil being taught and being received. This has been my view and opinion ever since.

By this time, I'd had enough of this life with Drake and filed for divorce after seven years of marriage. My attorney in the divorce provided me with enough funds to move to my home in Missouri, my seventy-five-acre farm. The move proved to be very short, less than a full year, for after much harassment and issues in that farm/ranch community, I was forced to leave and go back to California. I didn't know what else to do or where to go, so I packed up my stuff and regretfully headed back to the home I left behind, not knowing all that had taken place while I was gone. I failed again. Drake somehow got my home put into his name and withheld it from me. How it was done without my consent, I will never know. He had all the locks changed as I discovered when I arrived. My return was disappointing to say the least.

At this point of my returned to my house in California later in1982, I needed money to survive so I decided to try and raise poodles, for I was told by a friend of Drake's that his wife made real good money breeding and selling poodles. I knew nothing about poodles, except that they were cute. After looking in the newspapers under "dogs for sale," I found a person who had some pups. Mind you, I did not research what poodles are supposed to look like—in other words, their conformation and traits.

I bought two, for I thought they would be better off with a companion when I wasn't home. As they grew, their legs remained short. They looked like curly haired dachshunds instead of poodles. I then decided to go to a dog show to see what real poodles look like and inquired with some of them as to why my two dogs had short legs. They, for the most part, wouldn't even talk to me when they saw my two poodles. One breeder was "kind enough" to tell me I had bought into backyard junk and I would be better off just to put them down and start over or try some other form of companionship. I was very embarrassed and hurt. I did find a show person who would sell me one of her breed that was over the required confirmation size for a reduced price of five hundred dollars as long as I agreed to not breed the dog, which would ruin her breed name.

I eventually did get a better poodle and sold the original two I had acquired. Eventually, I had several beautiful, sweet, intelligent, loving dogs that did not bark over every little sound. I wondered if they could bark at all. I fell in love with them and spent a lot of time training them in obedience and being indoors. I did breed a few of them but was very picky about it and whom I sold them to. After all, they had become my children, so to speak!

My dogs helped me through a very rough time when I was sick in body and heart and felt I had nothing to live for since Elizabeth was gone. They kept me busy grooming them all—up to twenty-five pups at one time—giving them their shots, declawing, docking tails, etc. They were as beautiful as all the show dogs, but they didn't have to perform for anyone, except me. Later in my life there, I had to sell all of them, except two that eventually accompanied me across the States.

Drake and I left the Baptist church months after I returned from Missouri and joined a very large nondenominational church closer to home. They started a two-year Bible college, which I decided to participate in hopes of learning so much more and getting a degree in Bible theology. Drake was not interested and felt he knew all he needed to know. Four nights a week, I attended classes after work for two years and graduated but was never given a degree, for they had changed sponsors after the first year. I was extremely agitated and upset with them about that. It was extremely important for me to get that Bible theology degree at that time.

While attending that congregation of three-thousand-plus members, I had several spiritual encounters. One such encounter was during a Sunday service. We were sitting in the second row up front, out of our comfort zone, when we were told Pastor Baldwin and his wife were home with a midwife having their first child. I closed my eyes to pray, and I was suddenly transported in the spirit to the pastor's house in the room with him, his wife, and the midwife, sort of hovering over them, looking down. I was not alone but perceived that it was possibly an angel who took me there. We watched her baby boy being born.

Just as suddenly as I arrived there, I was back in the pew sitting next to Drake, and I woke up out of the spirit amazed and wanted to yell out, "It's a boy!" But I was kept from saying anything to anyone, except Drake. I told him what had just happened, and my words were not received. He did not believe me. Later in the service, it was announced that they had a boy.

We were now children leaders working with hundreds of children between six and twelve years of age at this church. What would happen if they even thought Drake was a possible child molester? At that time, I did not know just how severe the circumstances were with Elizabeth. The thought that Elizabeth had already been violated never came to me. My thought was I could lose my position in the church, my ministry license, my reputation. But even worse, how do I know that he did not molest or violate any children in our care? God forbid! Fortunately, Elizabeth was safely living with her father by this time and only visiting us on some weekends. I kept this deep dark secret to myself out of fear of rejection.

Another time while praying in the intercessory prayer group, I received a very detailed vision that I was to write on paper and bring it to the attention of the head pastor. I was shown many living cells pulsating and moving around yet connected to one another. Within the conglomeration of cells, some were broken apart by very black cells, a sort of cancer cell that was destroying the healthy cells. The Lord showed me this as the body of Christ and the congregation of that church. There were many healthy cells (people), but we were being invaded by the bad destroying cells. Perhaps Drake and I were one of those bad cells. I drew this out and presented it to the pastor as a warning of what was happening. He did not have much at all to say, and by the look on his face, I couldn't tell if he believed me or thought I was way out in left field.

Two months later, there was a church split, and two of the pastors left with some of the members. They were not missed by most of the people remaining, and life went on as usual in the congregation.

Then I understood those two pastors and their followers represented the bad cancer cells in the vision.

During our ministry at this church, we were very much into attending camps for adults and with the children we ministered to there. It was back in 1976 that I had the same dream and vison over and over in color of a godly Bible-based camp for restoration of souls. In my mind and heart, I wanted to help lost, hurting people, perhaps because I sensed I needed that myself. Only God knows the true intent of one's heart.

The full manifestation of this camp would encompass a minimum of two hundred acres, probably more. It consisted of nine leaders for nine departments or divisions: sports, prayer and worship, facilities, education, administration, cafeteria, agriculture, ranching, and machine shop. These nine leaders would run the camp under God's divine leadership.

The vision was quite detailed and included women, men, and staff's housing; medical house or clinic; retail store; various livestock stalls and pens; not to mention the various installations and equipment for recreation, sports, fishing, boating, and swimming pool. Every aspect was spelled out such as land preparation, crops, harvesting, food and grain storage, supplies, etc. It reminds me of the specifications God must have given Noah to build the ark. There is the main business-office building and a large dining room and cafeteria for all meals. Education was in the main building. We are talking about a lot of people running and operating this ranch and farm camp for many lost and hurting people. There was an area where cabins would be set up here and there in the designated camp area to rent to various approved church groups and private individuals (groups) to bring in finances for operation of the camp besides the outside donations and the items made by our residents sold in the camp store.

When all of the vision was put on paper, I laminated it and presented it to the leadership and members that were interested. The pastor and most leaders just thought it was an impossible pipe dream and asked me, "Who do you think you are?" This same scenario repeated itself in just about every church I attended. I was devastated, and even though a few members said they wanted to be a part of it, they looked to me for finances, organization, and development—for everything. This was never intended to be a one-person (me) development.

The drawings are still on my wall to this day as a reminder of what God can do in His time and if we are willing and able. God knew my marriage wasn't going to last. He knew where I would be in this day. Even though I am ready for His call, just as God told David that he would not be building His temple, but Solomon would be. I suppose God will select someone else to build the dream of this restoration property He has given me when He chooses at another time, for my life was not in order, and funding never came.

My mission has not changed since I received it in 1976: encourage abused, hopeless people to find their purpose in life; instruct and inspire them to develop skills to be productive in society and in their spiritual walk. In this large church we were attending, there were intercessory-prayer groups, healing groups, outside-ministry groups, and others of which I participated wholeheartedly. While learning Charles and Frances Hunter healing ministry, I witnessed and participated in many recoveries, saw and felt healings firsthand. The prayer group consisted of deep intercession on the floor with crying and wailing some time for several hours, getting results for the most part within our group. It taught me how to intercede for very long periods of time without ceasing. I certainly needed to intercede for myself, my marriage, and for Elizabeth, who was living with her dad.

During the second half of my marriage to Drake, I took up porcelain doll making. This was now January 1986, when I was already engulfed with my poodles. But I missed Elizabeth and thought taking doll-making classes would get her off my mind a bit. Besides, I enjoyed creating things from various mediums in art. It was very rewarding to branch out to sculpting faces with clay. Elizabeth still on my mind, I decided to make a porcelain doll in her image. I started with her face then decided to sculpt the rest of her body. It turned into a twenty-eight-inch doll, and by the time I put a wig on the doll, it was twenty-nine inches tall. I was so excited about the results. I showed her to my clay-sculpture teacher, who encouraged me to enter the Anaheim Doll Show in California. Boy, was I surprised to receive a second-place award for original doll out of about one hundred other entries in that category.

When I started bringing my dolls to show some of the people at my church congregation, some of the people became very dismayed about my doll making, throwing scripture at me and telling me I was doing work of the devil and should stop immediately or suffer the consequences of the wrath of God. "Stop sinning and return to God!" they would bark at me, while others thought it was a wonderful God-given talent and said they would be thrilled to have one of my creations. It left me perplexed, not knowing the full truth or understanding of God's Word on this matter. Was I doing the good and right thing, or was I really sinning? I continued making dolls and clothes of every size to fit each doll and was selling most of them. By 1988, all my remaining dolls were packed away and remained packed until 2018, when I finally settled into a peaceful place the Lord brought me to.

To my surprise, one of the pastors of this congregation came to Drake and me one day in 1986 with a proposition. There was a teenage boy named Carter, who needed a temporary home and had been passed around the families within the congregation for several years and had developed a lawless attitude with a very big chip on his shoulders. He wanted us to take the boy into our home, saying he thought it was a good fit, but I was very opposed, knowing our marriage was already on shaky ground. Drake liked the idea and persuaded the pastor to let him come and live with us. Strangely, Carter looked an awful lot like Drake, and they got along so well. For me, it turned sour, for Carter paid no attention to my house rules and requests, deliberately disobeying me to show me he could do anything he wanted. This went on for a few months while Drake would side with him on almost everything. At one point, I was concerned about the relationship between the two of them and how they both fought against me. Drake warned me not to push too far because he would choose Carter over me. Carter moved out eventually, or so it seemed, while I was living there.

After fourteen years living in an abusive, unhappy marriage with Drake, an event occurred again, which sent me over the edge this time: rape. I was so distraught, I gave in and told one of the ladies in the intersession group who was an assistant to the leaders. This woman confided in me that Sunday that three other families in the congregation had reported to her that they had living color dreams of Drake murdering me in detail, and she felt I should not attempt to go home with him but leave him immediately. So while Drake was watching me from a distance, talking to various people, arrangements were made for one of the couples who had the dream to come help me on Monday morning after Drake went to work. I was terrified to go home with him that afternoon, knowing what he had in store for me. When I escaped out of my home that Monday, I went into and remained in hiding by moving and changing jobs again. There were people taking me to church by meeting me at various places for pickup so that I would not be followed or arrive alone. Divorce was now imminent.

What is rape *to me?* I ask myself. It's giving up something very personal inside of me that I do not want to give up, taking or cutting away something personal by force against my will. Through all the years of my abuse, I learned to give in to the abuser or predator's demands to survive, losing myself. My response of *no* went unheard; my physical resistance and silent internal screams of fear or dislike against the abusers were not detected or acknowledged. After all, even the pastors and counselors said my body was not my own but that of my husband (when I was married). My will was of no importance, it seemed, and I hated my life.

During one of the remaining services I attended by myself, Drake was hiding in the parking lot near my parked truck, waiting for me to come out of the service. As soon as I opened the cab door, he came behind me and put his hand over my mouth, pushing me to get into the truck, bruising my legs and arms as I fought to get away. A family spotted us and came quickly to investigate. Drake was caught by surprise and let me go then decided to faint onto the ground. He was very good at faking, and I could only assume this was his way of getting favorable attention when caught abusing me. I ran into the church to get help.

This plan of my murder was never reported to authorities, for what tangible proof did I have? Who would report their vision to authorities, and who would believe them or me anyway? Although Drake had already purchased the tools needed to murder me and put me in the ground just as it was in the three couples' dreams revealed to me, it was not enough to suspect him of doing any evil against me according to the law.

When I turned thirty-five years old, supposedly mature enough to handle money, I received a small inheritance of thirty-five thousand dollars out of the 350,000 dollars from my grandparents' estate, which Drake knew I would be getting. I bought real estate in Missouri, a seventy-five-acre heavily wooded parcel with an old oak house with a large barn and a home in California, which we moved into. I was told a year after our divorce that my inheritance was the only reason he married me. He wanted the money, and I ended up losing it all one way or another. Drake had confessed this to a church member we both knew. I will not fret, for the Lord is in control and will do as He pleases in all things and situations for our good. I cried as I tried to convenience myself that God was in control.

> To the roots of the mountains I sank down; the earth beneath barred me in forever. But you brought my life up from the pit, O Lord my God. When my life was ebbing away, I remembered you, Lord, and my prayer rose to you, to your holy temple. ... Salvation comes from the Lord. (Jonah 2:6–7, 9 NIV)

> For the Word of God is alive and active. Sharper than any double-edged sword penetrates even to dividing soul and spirit, joints and marrow; it judges the thoughts and attitudes of the heart. Nothing in all creation is hidden from God's sight. Everything is uncovered and laid bare

before the eyes of him to whom we must give account. ...

Let us then approach God's throne of grace with confidence, so that we may receive mercy and find grace to help us in our time of need. (Hebrews 4:12–13, 16 NIV)

Now let me tell you of the miracle that happened in Hawaii.

CHAPTER 8

_____

Miracle in Hawaii

W hen Elizabeth was given to her dad to live in December 1981, I lost my purpose in life. She was the only living person who meant anything to me. She actually became my idol by my own hand. I did not believe I had any tangible relationship with God or Jesus or the Holy Spirit, whom people praised and talked about even though I was teaching in the church. I was not saved. I became so despondent, I sought to take my life again, for I felt there was nothing to live for.

I was still married in 1981 and living with Drake. It was toward evening, and I found myself in the corner of my kitchen floor against the cabinets with an ice pick in my hand, struggling to get the courage to plunge it into my heart, as I recounted in the previous chapter. Just as I was about to proceed, Drake came home from work and came into the kitchen and saw me and what I was about to do. He started laughing quietly at me and left the kitchen with a smile on his face. I was bewildered, and anger rose up in me. Suddenly, I realized how happy he would be if I went through with my death. No, no, I won't give him that pleasure, was my immediate thought, and at the same time, I heard a still, small voice inside of me, saying, *Go see Numan. Go see Numan in Hawaii.*

Why would I go see Numan? Why should I go see Numan? I thought, but without too much hesitation, I got up and called for an airline ticket to Hawaii for later that same week. Numan was Drake's relative, a literature teacher who used the Bible as his teaching tool. Upon arrival, in 1982, Numan alone was there to greet me at the airport. I was silent and stiff in the passenger seat, not knowing what to say on the drive to his home. His wife, Marsha, was there, and before we sat down to talk or get into any discussion, Numan asked me if I wanted to receive the Lord. I wasn't completely sure what that entailed since the Baptist church never had altar calls or calls for salvation, but I said yes. Nothing traumatic happened. No unusual feelings or emotion came on me as they prayed with the three of us holding hands together, quietly standing before the Lord for me to receive Jesus in my heart. I just repeated what they said and accepted Jesus in my heart. It was already afternoon when I looked up at the wall clock. When they were done praying, Marsha served lunch and some light, short discussion ensued.

Later that day, since they lived on the beach, I went for a walk on the beach. I felt invigorated. Everything seemed different. The colors of trees, sand, houses all looked so much more vibrant, alive. Barefoot, I walked along the shore. So refreshing it was. The sand was white and clean and felt so good under my feet. The sky was brilliant blue, and I heard voices, like angelic music, coming from between the sky and the sea. I thought it was my imagination. There was no one on the beach, no boom box, not anyone. I was happy and joyous for some reason. I verbally said, "I wish I could find some beautiful seashells," and before I finished speaking, I stubbed my toe on something. As I looked down, I saw it was a very beautiful shell, and right then, I knew God had heard me and provided it. Surely the angelic music I was hearing must have been angels in heaven rejoicing over my salvation. The sky was full of various brilliant colors of pink, orange, yellow, and greens as the afternoon sun was going down as a celebration of the close of a victorious day and the gentle wind caressing and blowing my hair about.

To my surprise, I had walked about five miles barefoot when I realized I had gone pretty far away from Numan's home. All the while, I witnessed the beauty of creation for the first time it seemed. *How come everything changed and looked so different?* I wondered.

I shared my adventure with Numan's family, and they explained God gave me different eyes to see His world as it was meant to be. Beyond that, there was no further explanation from them other than I am saved now, born again according to the Word of God. I never felt that well or free in my life up to that point.

After a week in Hawaii, I got back home, and everyone who knew me kept asking me, "What happened to you? Your countenance has changed. You look different."

I had no idea what they were talking about. I had no explanation. I merely said, "I received Jesus in my heart, I guess, and had a wonderful time." As yet, I had not noticed that I looked any different, but I felt different—a joy I had never experienced before. How sad that I could not put into words exactly what took place and tell them that they could have that same experience. *It was a miracle of God!*

No one in my family had ever received the Lord. There was no evidence at all of it. All the fears my grandparents put on me were just suddenly gone! I became a new person. Even Drake, my husband, who had been raised in the church, could not understand it. He became suspicious of me. Right off, I noticed most of the fear I was carrying was gone—no child-eating man in the drain sewer, no monster outside the window to devour me, total peace flying back home in turbulent weather. I felt renewed to start life all over again, leaving my old life behind. I wanted to stay longer to soak in this new life to the fullest but had to go back to a job waiting for me to return.

Shortly after arrival back in my hometown, I realized I had no desire to continue in the Baptist congregation or teach the children's program that had been established there. I did much repenting of the subject matter taught. I just knew I needed to know more, a different perspective, about God and Jesus. Sometime later, I found a nondenominational church much closer to our home and tried it out. I then convinced Drake to visit the church with me.

After a few weeks, we started going there regularly. They were planning to start an accredited (or so they said) ministry college, so

I decided to sign up for it and in 1983, started attending four or five evenings per week for the next two years. Drake was not interested in attending. What a joy it was to read and learn the Word of God. Upon graduation two years later, those working on staff were all ordained as ministers of the Word, including myself, even though I did not feel I was called. Upon graduation, I discovered it really was not an accredited college as they said it was going to be. What a huge disappointment for me. Did they really lie to us? I received a diploma for each year completed and framed them.

The church leaders had hired me as an accounting assistant in the finance department, and I also started working with the children's ministry under the children's pastor. I loved it so much that I spent almost all of my time in church. There was nothing for me to go home to until I fell in love with a couple of poodles I purchased. Soon I had a house full of poodles, which kept me busy grooming and training them.

As often as I could, I would give my testimony of salvation and how it had changed me. Truthfully, though, I was still not free of the past hurts, scars, and demons, and they manifested from time to time in word or deed. My mind was being renewed but at a very slow pace. My actions still did not always prove to be Christian. Once I threw all of Drake's prized possessions in a dumpster believing I was cleaning my house of evil spirits as per instructions from some well-meaning Bible teachers in the congregation. I did not consult Drake about it until after the fact, and you have to know that did not go well at all. Unknown to me, I still had a lot to learn and a lot from which to recover. Yet it was exciting to learn what God had to say. I had kept all of my books and teaching tapes over those two years of class. My living conditions and marriage remained in turbulence to my dismay.

The desire to help people was so strong that I got training to be a lay chaplain minister so I could go to hospitals and pray over patients. I also got a position with a nursing home, visiting patients once a week with conversation and prayer. After a year of seeing people die there, I gave it up, for it was too much to deal with along with a failing marriage.

I discovered I could go up and down stairs and high places now without thinking about it. In fact, one summer, I was alone on my farm in Missouri, and I had to climb up on the roof to clean out the chimney. It was a glorious moment of triumph being able to do that all by myself without fear. My life had become full. No more loneliness no matter where I was, in a crowd or by myself at home. I was filled with peace as I understood it then and joy within me most of the time. When I flew back from Hawaii, it was very stormy conditions. The plane was greatly kicked about and took a few nosedives that made me think about dying. I realized I wasn't afraid of death any longer, for I knew for sure that I would go to heaven. I had such peace about it!

The reality was that I still had to live with an abusive, cheating husband. He was an embarrassment to me. I still had to work with the same distrusting people. I still had the same friends who claimed to be Christians (many) who did not appear to be living that so-called Christian life. What made the difference for me was that now I had someone to go to for help, someone who seemed to be with me in times of trouble: my friend Jesus, who helped me even though I could not see or hear Him doing His work on my behalf. I no longer wanted to socialize with the same friends, for I found they hampered my progress with the Lord, pulling me back into old patterns of behavior.

I learned that when we keep our hearts soft, we can hear and feel God leading us and feel His presence. Someone with a hard heart can't feel anything but his own suffering and discomfort. Our tongue gives us away. At this point, I was just beginning to understand the power of the tongue and how I had been speaking evil and not much good over myself and others. It seemed to come naturally. I thought I had finally made it, only to be disappointed again. My heart was still hard from all my years of abuse and still living in that abuse. I found it hard to forgive and was not really sure how to forgive.

Nevertheless, I told myself I was happier than ever before and that I just needed to work hard at everything I did, not realizing I still needed deliverance from generational curses and demons, which had accumulated in our home. With the teaching I had received, I fought the good fight of faith to the best of my ability. It just wasn't enough. There was more to be done, and looking back, the Lord was leading me toward His goal, His plan for my life.

The very first time the Bible ever spoke to me was back in the Baptist church in a different two-year evening Bible class. I was still unsaved then. These words came off the page and into my heart with great surprise and pleasure:

> "For I know the plans that I have for you," declares the Lord, "plans for welfare and not for calamity to give you a future and a hope. Then you will call upon me and come and pray to Me and I will listen to you. You will seek Me and find Me when you search for Me with all your heart. I will be found by you," declares the Lord, "and I will restore your fortunes and will gather you from all the nations and from places where I have driven you," declares the Lord, "and I will bring you back to the place from where I sent you into exile." (Jeremiah 29:11–14 NASB)

> See, I have appointed you this day over the nations and over the kingdoms, to pluck up and to break down, to destroy and to overthrow, to build and to plant. (Jeremiah 1:10 NASB)

> Before I formed you in the womb I knew you. And before you were born I consecrated you; I have appointed you a prophet to the nations. (Jeremiah 1:5 NASB)

While reading and after reading these scriptures, I got goose bumps all over, for I was so taken back. His Word jumped into my soul. These scriptures became alive to me and spoke to me personally. But surely they are not meant for me. After all, who am I really? I am a nobody! Nevertheless, I received His words into my heart and quietly pondered on them through the years. My life was changing by His Word, slowly, quietly, for good.

Truly, my salvation, a life-changing experience in Hawaii, was a *miracle of God!*

CHAPTER 9

Voice of God

n April 1982, after seven years of marriage to Drake, I filed for divorce. This was shortly after the miracle in Hawaii and after Elizabeth was gone from me. I loaded up my truck and U-Haul and headed for Missouri, where I had previously purchased a seventy-five-acre farm in the Ozarkian Hills, as I called it. It had an old oak wood frame house with uneven floors and a number of rooms that were not quite distinguishable as to their use. There was an indoor toilet in the bathroom, but it was connected to a septic hole in the ground about fifty feet south from the house, which apparently had never been cleaned out or emptied. There was no flushing for a time! The kitchen was distinguishable only by a broken-down stove and old refrigerator. Many of the rooms did not have Sheetrock on the walls, and the bare frame was exposed. Fortunately, the house had a very large attic but no stairs to get up to it, for it had not been used as living space.

I had walked the entire perimeter or boundaries of the property and found good fencing throughout. The property bordered much larger parcels over hundreds of acres, which were mostly plowed and planted. The wildlife would come through my property, for it was heavily wooded and gave protection and food to the critters as they leisurely meandered through. I remember the first week I moved in the property, a family of large deer came slowly walking down the dirt driveway to cross over and forage along the way. As they passed by my bedroom window, one deer, the largest one, had antlers that looked to be about four or more feet across. Wow! What a spectacular sight to see! He spotted me looking at him through the window and just stopped and stared at me for a few seconds then resumed his leisurely walk, for apparently, I did not seem a threat to him or his flock.

Another time, a very large old turtle, about two or more feet long, strolled down the drive to the spring-fed pond in the backyard. Never had I seen such a thing. What a glorious time it was to observe nature in the wild and picking wild berries that grew throughout the property.

The first two days after I arrived, there was a warning of tornados and to take cover, which I never got because I had no Internet. The house did not have locks on the doors or windows, so the first night, I put a chair up under the front doorknob and being exhausted, I crawled into bed and slept very soundly.

The next morning, I was awakened by a truck horn barreling down my dirt drive and people in the truck shouting something. I jumped out of bed to find it was the neighbors anxious to see if I had survived the tornado, yelling the tornado tore through their property and some of the other neighbors. I said it never even woke me up, and we looked around and found the tornado had not touched my property at all, not even a single tree! It skipped me entirely. I thought it was possibly God watching out for me and stated so, but they didn't comprehend that if there was a God, He would do such a thing and just laughed me off as a joke. It made them all the more upset since their property was hit, but I didn't realize that at that moment. They were quite bewildered as they left me and headed back to their home right next door, about a quarter mile down the road.

Since I was a fairly new Christian having just been saved, I was listening to a Christian radio station, wanting to learn more about God's Word and what I should do with my life. It was evening, and I heard voices shouting and some gunfire way out in the woods behind the house. When I looked to see what was happening, I saw lights from lanterns or flashlights. The speaker on the radio was talking about end times. At that moment I panicked, for I had just heard the story of the ten virgins, five of whom had oil for their lanterns and five who did not and were left behind. My thoughts raced, knowing I had not bought any oil for my one and only lantern. *Oh, no, what am I going to do?* I thought to myself in a panic. *Now I am in trouble and will surely be left behind*, was my thinking, for I still did not understand the full meaning of the Scriptures. As it turned out, men were hunting or looking for something, and it was not the end of days, but the very next day I went and bought oil for my lantern, for I did not want to be left behind. I had a lot to learn!

Before I left California, my attorney arranged for me to get around twenty thousand dollars from the divorce settlement, which was still in progress. I used much of the money to fix the house, remodeling the kitchen and attic, to make it more livable. I had a staircase built to go up to the attic to put in walls, ceiling, and new blue carpet. I painted the upper bedroom walls pink. My thought was that I wanted to get Elizabeth to come stay with me, and she would have the entire large attic all to herself. So I hired a handyman to get started on renovations to this old oak house right away.

I was not yet working at the time, and it was spring time, so I decided to put in a thirty-by-fifty-foot garden about two hundred feet from the home next to the big barn. On my hands and knees, I harvested every size rock imaginable for days and used them to make a border around the garden. The neighbors helped rototill the plot. Excitement and anticipation arose in me while I was planting all the seeds, thanking God for His bounty and the beauty of the land He has given to mankind. It took many days to complete, but it was the thrill of putting my bare hands in the dirt, the smell of the earth, and anticipation of homegrown food. My poodles must have thought I was nuts, for they watched me from the covered porch. One of them, however, loved me so much, she came and lay down next to me on the dirt in pouring rain one day. She made me feel so sorry for her, I had to stop planting and go inside and dry her off.

The twenty thousand dollars was running out, so I decided to get my oil paints and canvases and go on the arts-and-crafts circuit in Branson, Missouri, and wherever a craft show cropped up. I would set up my easel and canvas and started painting. People interested would gather around and watch me paint until the painting was done. Someone would always pay the one-hundred-dollar price and walk off with the wet painting. Other times, I'd do a commissioned painting for a price. It gave me food and gas money and pleasure in creating something special for people.

Eventually, Elizabeth arrived after she received my round-trip airline ticket. I was so elated. *I finally got her back!* My dream of us being together here was coming true. I cashed in her return ticket without telling her, for in my mind, I thought she would love this place and surely stay. She did love the farm and her private upstairs abode as well as the meadows she played in. I got her a horse named Dugar, which she promptly mounted and rode off bareback, scaring me as I didn't know if she could handle the horse. She had learned how to ride at summer camp I sent her to years earlier.

The property had a large meadow beyond the barn laced with every kind of wild flower one could imagine. It was beautiful and very quickly became Elizabeth's favorite place to roam. Butterflies and birds frequented the place for the wild flowers colors, aromas, and nectar. There was so much to see and explore on this seventy-five-acre farm. We were experiencing closeness to God without realizing it. It was so exhilarating and beautiful.

I had purchased some goats, chickens, and rabbits from a family I met at a church I attended, so I had a good supply of eggs, meat, and milk. Somehow, Elizabeth and a new neighbor friend she acquired let the goats get out of their pen. Two of the goats saw the open door of the house and ran inside from room to room, girls chasing and yelling behind them to stop. The goats jumped back and forth on the beds and anything else they could get onto to escape the crazy screaming girls. I was so angry, but at the same time, it was hysterical to watch. What a mess! The two goats were finally caught and put back in the pen, but I was left with cleaning up the mess.

There was a river down the way with a low bridge crossing over it where the local folk would go to cool off on hot summer days. We went a few times and loved it, still being very careful to watch for water moccasins. Some folk would throw out a line to fish. It was those wonderful, laid-back summer days you only dream of and see in the movies. We treasured that time spent there. At those times, there was no burden or undue care. The time was passing too quickly as far as I was concerned. Great memories were made there.

It was time for Elizabeth to go back. She had been counting the days. When I told her I wanted her to stay and that I got a refund on the ticket, she was furious with me. She said in no uncertain terms she did not want to live with me and wanted to go home, so I reluctantly accommodated her desire and took her to the airport in silence. My mind was racing in every direction, trying to come up with some way to have her stay. Her mind was made up. She was not turning back! She boarded the plane without hesitation, not even looking back at me. My heart sank, and it felt like my life—my future—was slipping away again. I watched in horror as the only person I loved got in that big 747 and taxied down the runway, getting ready for takeoff. Then lifting up, it slowly disappeared into the blue sky and clouds, my dreams and hope with it.

Suddenly, an explosion of loud, deep, heavy sobs came forth from me, and I was unable to control my emotions. The thought of losing her again, probably forever, was just more than I could bear. The plane took off—up, up into the air. No one except me cared. I walked quickly to my truck, sobbing loudly while people were turning to see where the loud crying was coming from. I could not stop the enormous flood of uncontrollable emotion of loud crying as I walked to my parked truck outside the terminal. I could barely see where I was going through the streaming tears.

When I got to my truck, I opened the door of the cab, and as I was getting in, immediately at that very moment, a calm, normal, *audible voice* came from inside the cab, saying, "Give her to Me. I know every hair on her head. Give her to Me."

Stunned, I looked to see who that was. At the same time, my sobs completely stopped. No one was there! I knew in my heart God had just spoken to me—no doubt! A strange sense of peace fell on me, and I knew He was going to take care of her better than I ever could. I missed her and wanted her for myself, but now I had peace that she was in *His* hands. Yet there was an overwhelming sense of loss that came over me, not knowing what to do now. I had planned all this for *us*, for a new beginning, a new life together. It just came to an abrupt end, yet having heard the *voice of God*, I kept that strange sense of peace within me. In life, there are times we have to let go of those we love. Only in faith can we have them back at God's appointed time, not ours, as I have learned the hard way. Brokenhearted, I drove toward home, wondering what I would do now.

God allowed defeat and disappointment in my life to prepare me for the future, to serve His purposes, His plans. So when my dreams came crashing down on me, I needed to not despair. God is in control. I believe that God wanted to prepare me to do things His way instead of doing things my way, which did not glorify Him. *His* way is always better. It is not always easy to surrender to His ways as I found out.

Since I had renovated the oak house to make it bigger and more comfortable, my thoughts turned to being a foster parent to children in town of mixed race whom no one wanted, who were in desperate need of a temporary place while Children's Social Services found permanent adoptive homes for them, now that Elizabeth left. I mentioned this to one of my neighbors and was extremely disturbed by his response. He said if I took in any Negro or mixed-race kid, he'd burn my house down. "We don't want that kind here."

This very same neighbor moved his fence over about ten or more feet onto my property without discussing or asking me about it. When I caught him and his sons in the act of tearing down my fence and putting his up on my land, he simply said he was "claiming his land." I felt too alone and vulnerable against an unscrupulous gun-toting person in very rural countryside to do anything about it at the time, and I knew the other neighbors were not going to help me make it right. By this time, they viewed me as a sinful divorcee.

When my property would be sold, I imagined a new survey would surely be taken and borders would be rectified. However, his comment about the children I wanted to take in put a thick wall or resentment and disgust in me against him. Eventually, I had to forgive him in my heart and let God do His work on this man and his family. Years later, I learned the house that I renovated was burned to the ground. By whom, I never found out.

One of my neighbors, a strict Baptist preacher, told me I had no right to leave Drake, and I needed to go back home to him where I belonged. He kept pestering me about it and used me as a negative example to his congregation as a "woman gone astray." The neighbors had turned against me by this time. If I had more faith and understanding of how to proceed in life, particularly in that environment of rural-country dwellers, I might have chosen to stick it out. The nearest store was Skutto, six miles away, which was our post office, general store, and gas station—an all-in-one shopping center. The nearest town was Evon, Mo., approximately fifteen miles north. The area was awesomely beautiful and serene, something you would see in the travel magazines. I loved it and wanted to retire there. Reluctantly, I packed up and went back to California to the *house* I left behind for seven more years of what turned out to be more hell for me.

The one family that I stayed friends with and enjoyed, who sold me their goats and other animals and taught me some rural living functions, had hoped I would stay despite anyone else's opinion. They cared for me and taught me a lot. Not too many months later, they had to make a move out of state for other reasons. We kept in touch for a few years until my life got more chaotic. I just quit writing them letters due to my messed-up life being an embarrassment to me.

Only recently have I learned that people who come against you are there for a reason: to move you into the place God wants you to be, even if it's by pure agitation. My path or your path or road in life may not be smooth or straightforward. Mine certainly was not. God doesn't always take you on a straight path on purpose. The closed doors or wrongs imposed on you by people—the hurts, discouragements, and suffering—are at times strategically controlled by God to get you where God wants you to be.

We are a very stubborn people sometimes, not willing to budge or move, or we want to go our own direction, so God many times must redirect us using people to be the obstacle in the way of our own plans. Just as God had to redirect the Hebrews in the dessert for forty years instead of taking them on a direct path to the promised land, for they were not ready to cope or receive.

The problems are not there to defeat you, although it may feel that way at times, but they are there to take you to higher ground, to move you where He wants you to be. Yes, sometimes it feels like we have to go through the fire, but in so doing, we become refined, and the bad or undesirable is burned off. Bless those people who agitate or rub you the wrong way, for they have been placed in your path for a reason. It may be difficult, but see them as a sign from God working in your behalf. Yes, I know that's a very difficult thing to do sometimes, but God will see you through it. Just ask for His help.

> God disciplines us for our good, in order that we may share in his holiness. No discipline seems pleasant at the time, but painful. Later on, however, it produces a harvest of righteousness and peace for those who have been trained by it. Therefore, strengthen your feeble arms and weak knees. Make level paths for your feet, so that the lame may not be disabled, but rather healed. (Hebrews 12:10–13 NIV)

> For Satan himself masquerades as an angel of light. It is not surprising, then, if his servants also masquerades as servants of righteousness. Their end will be what their actions deserve. (2 Corinthians 11:14–15 NIV)

> Then the Lord spoke to you out of the fire. You heard the sound of words but saw no form; there was only a voice. (Deuteronomy 4:12 NIV)

CHAPTER 10

Face-to-Face with China

W hen I arrived back in California from Missouri, I reluctantly settled back into the house with Drake. We continued going to the Baptist church until early 1983. It was not a very happy reunion for me. I found work as a bookkeeper for some interior decorators, a couple who rented a building with another group of some religious organization. Their office was, as expected, filled with raw material samples, decorative items, sample books, etc. The couple was dressed as expected as home decorators and put on airs of being well-to-do.

When they showed me the rest of the building we would have to pass through to get to the restrooms, I was taken aback. There was a foreboding large dark type of a room with no windows, with an elaborate very large, oversized chair placed up high on a platform or stage as though it was a throne. There was elaborate trimming all around it. I got goose bumps, and the hair on my arms stood straight up, not at all like what I felt when I read the Bible and His words came alive. This felt like pure evil.

I decided I would not be going to the bathroom at all. I needed the job for the finances and took it. Of course, the force of nature does have its way from time to time, but all was done in record time in those dark moments passing through that dark evil room.

The couple had not been keeping financial records or reconciling their bank accounts, so that was the first thing I had to do. I went back five years and started reconstructing and recording their expenditures and income and reconciling their bank statements. It was a daunting task, but I loved doing the work to resolve accounting issues.

Very quickly, it came to me that I needed to pray over the demons in the building, for I could feel the presence of evil walking around me. Having read various accounts in the Word of God, I decided to follow the plan God gave Joshua to conquer Jericho. I told Drake of my plan. He refused to take part in it, but he drove me to the location and waited in the car late at night, believing or suspiciously thinking I was planning to do something else. Just as Joshua marched around Jericho, by myself, I marched around this evil-filled building seven times, praying in the Spirit for the Lord to knock down the walls of evil. Because of Drake, I was only allowed to walk and pray that one night, seven times around in the dark of night, alone praying in the spirit.

Well, the building did not fall down. I didn't pray for the building to fall down. I prayed for the Lord to expel the evil. By this time, I had worked the couple's financials enough to know they were in deep financial trouble. At one point, I was concerned where they were going to get the money to pay my salary.

Within two weeks of walking around the building, several men came into the building looking for the couple. They looked like detectives but produced badges and ID, stating they were from the IRS. The couple had not paid taxes for the last five years and owed big time. They confiscated books and data, and after I explained who I was and why I was there, they told me they were closing down the building, the business, and locking it up! So I had to take my own possessions and leave the job immediately. My intercession or prayers, like Joshua's, was not in vain. God prevailed. Of course, I lost my job and never got paid, and the couple never tried to contact me to pay my wages. I wonder what ever happened to them. Nevertheless, God had the victory over the enemy.

Life was going on as usual for me—a struggle with Drake. There were times when life seemed to be going just okay, but neither of us was very happy. One evening, I was coming back from a church meeting. When I turned down a particular street near home, I saw a speeding car driving away from an accident. It was a hit-and-run. A young man looking to be in his twenties was on the ground near a bent up bicycle. The man was groaning, and blood was all over his face and hands. I had to make a split-second decision: go after the car I saw speeding away or take care of the young man. I stayed with him but did not have CPR or first aid training. He begged me not to call an ambulance or take him to the hospital. Apparently, he had little or no finances. What else could I do but get him in my car and take him to my home?

Drake had told me he knew CPR and had first aid training. When I arrived, I ran in to tell Drake what had happened and to help this young man. He became furious that I would bring this man to our home. He refused to help him. Instead, he angrily grabbed the keys to the car out of my hand and drove him to a hospital, or so I was told. Drake refused to talk to me when he came back. He was still infuriated with me for getting involved. What could I have possibly done wrong?

My spirit grieved. My mind went back to my grandparents in Italy when they left a man who was struck down to die in the road. We have become so callous in regard to life, to each other. There seems to be little regard for human life. Respect has lost its way, even within the Christian communities, for the most part. What ever happened to "love your neighbor"? It truly grieves me when things like this happen. I had to try to let God handle it at that point, for I had made very little restoration in my relationship with Drake. Most of the time, there was little or no conversation between us. I could only hope and believe that God took care of the young man.

After searching for work again, I found a part-time girl Friday position with several Asian real estate brokers. I was the only white person and the only female in their office. They had several realtors, all of whom spoke in their native tongue most of the time. One of the young men, Lam, was bigger in size and taller than all of the others, seemingly out of conformation. I never knew what they were saying but guessed they were talking about me and laughing a lot by their turning heads to look or stare at me, probably wondering why Jason, one of the brokers, hired me. Eventually, it became full-time work. I paid no mind to them and did my work to the best of my ability, happy that I was working in real estate.

After working there for some time, I took a trip to Hawaii, hearing that still, small voice one day in my desperation with Drake. That is when I was born again, giving me a renewed spirit to work with God, knowing He had placed me there with this company for His reasons, unknown to me then.

Jason had several run-down apartments in the next city, which he rented out to immigrants (legal or not) from Asia, strictly on a cash basis. Jason dressed very expensively and did not like to go collect his rent from these tenants for fear they may assault him and take his money or even worse, kill him and throw him down the ravine where he would not be found. He asked me one day if I would please go for him and only collect cash. He failed to tell me of any possible danger until months later. Of course, I went.

When I arrived, it was like arriving in another country. Some of the people were cooking food outside on the grass. Some had a wood-burning fire on top of the electric stove. Most did not have beds, merely a mat rolled out on the floor. No one had showed them how to use the electric appliances or the plumbing. What a mess! They were hungry and asked if I had any food. Of course, only a few knew a little English.

My heart went out to them. I started delivering food to them once a month until Jason finally told me they would not hesitate to harm me if they ever became disgruntled with me. I quit going there altogether and prayed the Lord would send help to them, like the Health Department or Human Services or some county agency to help them, at least show them how to use the appliances and plumbing. *Why didn't Jason teach them modern living?* I wondered. It appeared to me that he ran his properties like a slumlord.

Lam befriended me and spoke of his native people in Vietnam and Laos, telling me how sad the situation was over there and explaining how poor and destitute they were. He explained that they were farmers but lacked necessary food to eat and fertilizers to make seeds grow well enough to supply them with adequate produce for consumption. Week after week, he would tell me these kinds of stories. Then one day, he said he found an ingredient here in the US that would greatly improve the farming back in Vietnam and surrounding countries, but because his English was insufficient to make calls around the US to possible suppliers, he asked if I would help him.

By this time, he had taken me on business trips to a couple of Asian restaurants in San Francisco to taste their cuisine as an example of what they eat and grow and to discuss the issue. One restaurant was very dark, with the only light coming from the windows located about twenty feet above the floor, a warehouse environment. There were very small round bowls with a lit candle inside at each small table. All I could see was the same round tan faces in dark clothing, about two hundred of them, seated at the tables. It was a little eerie, and I was the only white person there. I felt like an intruder, especially when they would glance at me with not-so-friendly faces, and the food was foreign to me, not much to my liking.

After thinking briefly about helping him find this product he wanted and supposedly needed, I agreed to help him. From his pocket, he produced a small plastic bag with small white beads, larger than grains of sand, and called it urea. He told me the kind of places I needed to call to procure the ingredient.

So now I thought I had a wonderful mission to help poor, deprived people get a better life, supplying them with this valuable fertilizer called Urea. I never prayed or asked the Lord about this, I just assumed it was from the Lord. Before and after work, I would make calls all over the US to syndicates who, after a time, claimed to know who I was, and within two months, I found a supplier.

This is when things really became weird. Lam made appointments to meet his fellow countrymen in San Francisco (in the underground areas of Chinatown). We first met a couple of men downtown dressed in trench coats, hats, and sunglasses who motioned

Lam and me into the back seat of their car and drove us to another location, which was the basement of a florist shop in Chinatown. There we met with two more men dressed in dark trench coats, hats, and sunglasses. All of us then walked down a San Francisco street to another location. As we were walking, I was behind them with Lam, and I was laughing quietly inside myself because it reminded me of *James Bond* movies of mysterious encounters in the underworld. Here I am, a tall redhead walking with what looked like secret agents in Chinatown. I had hoped my stupid grin was not showing.

Finally, we met a couple more men and drove off in two cars to another location, a restaurant. Again, there was very low lighting, and we were ushered to an upper room. When they opened the double doors, I freaked out. There, seated around an enormous round table, were Chinese military men in maroon-red uniforms, hats, and dirty-gold trim. Their faces were all grim, scary to me. Lam had warned me earlier not to speak, to stay quiet. I was face-to-face with China's military men. I never uttered a word. I was too frightened, trying to figure out what China's military had to do with anything.

The meeting lasted about twenty very long minutes, in which my name was mentioned, and a couple of the men nodded my way. I was so relieved when the meeting was dismissed and we all left but was confused and perplexed about the Chinese military. What did they have to do with this? What were they really discussing all that time? Why had I not been told they would be there? My amusement and the laughing within me was completely gone, leaving me with questions and uncertainty. I was quite perplexed and ill at ease by this time.

Lam then told me for the first time after the meeting that there was millions of dollars involved, and I would be rewarded greatly, but not to mention this meeting to anyone. All this time, he had not mentioned any payment of money, and I never expected to get paid for voluntary missionary work anyway. But the very next business weekday, I went to see the head pastor of the large congregation I was attending and told him everything and that I would like to donate the money I would be getting to the church. Instead of being elated, he had a concerned look on his face. He said his close friend in the church was staying up late at night making calls around the US looking for the same thing, hoping to strike it rich but so far was unsuccessful, causing much grief to his family and friends and the pastor himself. He strongly suggested I go see his attorney right away before I did anything else and handed me his attorney's card. I was even more perplexed. Why wasn't he excited about getting lots of money or the wonderful work I was doing?

The very next day, I called his attorney, who said he would see me right away. I was met with another concerned straight face. After repeating what I had told my pastor, he asked me if I knew what urea was. I said, "Yes, it's a type of fertilizer." His reply was that it could be used as a fertilizer but generally is not. He explained further that urea is used in warfare for producing bombs, etc., for war. At that very moment, I felt blood draining from my body and my head and thought I was going to collapse on the floor. I had been lied to again—duped, made a fool of. The attorney further said the US government could consider my actions to be treason, and I could go to jail. He advised me to drop my mission immediately.

At that very hour, I did just that as I was extremely shaken to the core. Now I understood the reason the Chinese military was at hand. I trusted Lam and fell for his lies. Now I may be in trouble. Where was God in all this? Was I so consumed in doing "my mission," "my thing" that I was not listening to Him? I never thought He would let me go astray. Did I even ask God about what I was doing? No, I didn't. I just made an assumption based on "good works" (?) that this was His plan for me. How foolish and immature of me to assume anything good would come of this now-very-stupid venture I called a "mission from God." Lied to again. When will I ever learn?

The following Sunday, the pastor's friend saw me in the congregation and came hurriedly to me, grabbing my arm and pulling me, shouting at me, "Give me the name! Give me the number! Give it to me!" He wanted the information I had acquired from the syndicate.

Immediately, three or four ushers came running to grab him, taking his grip off of me. It took all three men to subdue him and take him away while he was cursing at me. I never saw him again during the remaining short weeks I attended that church. No matter who you are or what position you may have in a religious or secular organization, we are still susceptible to the devil's schemes and lies once we take our eyes off of our Maker. We cannot live for money and live for Christ at the same time. It's one or the other. My heart was fixed on helping the poor and suffering people until the money came into focus at the very end yet still not understanding it was a deception of Satan.

Fear gripped me. By this time, late 1987, I had left Drake and was in the process of divorce again, for seven more years had gone by. Without asking God, again, I made a split decision to quit my job immediately with the Asian real estate company and at the same time, to physically move to an undisclosed location, to go into hiding. Fear had taken over again. I still had Lam's urea packet, and I decided to throw it in a dumpster, anywhere. I found a bookkeeping position with another broker-realtor in another city and was given permission to sleep in my truck and trailer in the parking lot of his company's property until one of his apartments became available. My two poodles were still with me, and they hated being kept in that little camper, but I had trained them well.

When one of his apartments did open up, I moved in but only stayed a few months. I had no furniture, but the Lord blessed me in abundance with everything I could possibly need or use—and all for free. I had failed to seek God out in my actions and decisions, yet He still blessed me and provided for me as He had always done before. He heard my cry for help. He knew my heart, but I had just not recognized His hand over me until then.

Looking back, I realize God gives us freedom to make our own decisions with or without Him. When we make the wrong decisions, He is still there watching over us but allows us to reap what we have sown, the consequences of our actions. He is a loving God but is also a just God, only allowing as much judgment as we can endure at a time. He is a parent, my parent, who seeks to show me and others the path, the way I should go. If only I would seek Him out and learn how to hear His direction all the time. He is very forgiving but allows us to suffer the consequences of our actions—as I did—to grow into a mature, responsible adult the way He desires His children to go. When will I learn to seek Him out?

I was greatly disheartened by what I had done and what came of my actions. I had failed again and was tired of looking over my shoulders to see if anyone was following me. So in my regrets and sorrow, I decided to move again, this time to get out of California to where my daughter was now living in Oklahoma. After I had left Drake, I flew to Oklahoma and purchased property with the thought of living there and returned for a short time, not realizing I would be leaving California sooner than I had planned.

> Not by way of eye service, as men-pleasers, but as slaves of Christ, doing the will of God from the heart. With good will render service, as to the Lord, and not to men, knowing that whatever good thing each one does, this he will receive back from the Lord, whether slave or free. (Ephesians 6:6–8 NASB, Works)

> He has not dealt with us according to our sins, nor rewarded us according to our iniquities. For as high as the heavens are above the earth, so great is His lovingkindness toward those who fear Him. As far as the east is from the west, so far has He removed our transgressions from us. Just as a father has compassion on his children, so the Lord has compassion on those who fear Him. (Psalm 103:10–13 NASB, condemnation)

CHAPTER 11

Escape from Egypt?

My life up to November 1988 had been very hurtful and laborious, one of much suffering. I felt like a slave with a brutal master—many brutal masters—controlling me with one lie after another. Having to continually look over my shoulder and rearview mirror of my car for the enemy who may be following me when I drove or walked around the city. I decided I couldn't take it any longer. The Israelites, originally called Hebrews, became slaves forced to make dry bricks (forced heavy labor) for the Egyptians under a brutal taskmaster called Pharaoh, and they did not see any way out of their entrapment. Even though they outnumbered the Egyptians, slavery was all they knew after four hundred years of enslavement. My feelings of being enslaved by ungodly people brought me to the realization I should escape my own entrapment, escape from my very own Egypt—California!

I called friends at the new church I was attending for help moving and ended up giving almost everything I acquired those short months away to the church. During the marriage to Drake, I purchased a brand-new three-quarter-ton pickup truck and got it completely paid off. When I knew I was leaving California, I had five hundred dollars of work done to the engine to improve hauling capacity across the states.

Out of boredom one day, I went looking at new cars at a dealership, for I considered it free entertainment and fun. As I arrived at this particular dealership, a salesperson asked me for the keys to the truck to see how much it would be worth as a trade-in. I thought, *Oh, why not? It would be good information*, while another salesman took me on a test-drive of a van I showed interest in. Mind you, I was just trying to have some free fun, which I had not been experiencing. The dealership confiscated my truck and hid it in the back lot, and I was manipulated into getting a vehicle I could not afford. They would not even let me see my truck for the last time.

Later, I found this trickery, as I call it, to be legal in California. I ended up towing my new van on a dolly behind a large and very old U-Haul truck, the only one available at that time, which had a clutch and long stick shift with a handle in the middle of the floor. It seemed I must have had a sign on my back with the words *sucker, victim, gullible, idiot girl,* or some other detestable name describing me for a very long time. Remorse set in.

It was winter 1988 and very cold. After studying the US maps, I took off with my two remaining poodles, my new van towed behind the old U-Haul truck, and headed for Bent Oak, Oklahoma. A month earlier, I had purchased property there and decided I might as well go live there to be closer to my daughter, who was attending ORU. Well, as I was attempting to leave, the van came loose from the trailer it was on, twice, so that I had to stop and get help to secure it. Then the trailer came loose from the truck! Again, I needed help. There were spiritual chains that bound me there in California, trying to keep me from escaping. There was an eerie, tangible presence around me, like evil spirits.

Crossing over the California-Arizona border was a miracle in itself! As I crossed over the border, it seemed the spiritual chains suddenly broke loose, and the eerie presence was gone. The truck picked up speed, and there were no more problems with the vehicles until I got to New Mexico. I pulled into a motel overnight and found it snowed all night. Morning had come, and I had to get a road construction worker to turn the truck around to get out of the parking lot because the truck would not go in reverse. Surprise, surprise! I never learned how to drive on ice or snow, having spent most of my life in California. So knowing the truck had no reverse and the weather forecast was for more snow, I chose to brave the road to Oklahoma anyway instead of being stuck there for who knows who long. It was not fun at all driving that bulky truck in snow and ice. I actually asked God to help me!

Finally arriving in Bent Oak, Oklahoma, to my homes, with much anticipation for a new life, no one was there to greet me. I had two homes on one corner property. I had thought Elizabeth would be there, but the homes were empty and very cold. She had not moved in and was living elsewhere. With help from my new neighbors, I eventually settled into one of the houses and started scouring the newspapers for work. Unfortunately, the weather became icy with one- to two-foot snowdrifts. I thought, *I have made it this far. I am going to drive anyway. I can do this!*

I managed to get out of the driveway and a block down the road toward the stop sign intersecting a very busy street. I stepped on the brake, but the van just kept going until it slammed sideways into a snowdrift, hitting a curb. Very meekly and terrified, I slowly turned the van around and maneuvered it back into my driveway with my heart pounding ninety miles a minute. I'd have to live on crackers and water until the snow melted, I decided half-heartedly. That was very discouraging, but I made the best of it, getting settled into the house and staying warm.

A week or so later, the roads were clear. However, to my disappointment, I discovered employers were not hiring people who had just moved in from out of state. I again scoured the newspapers and found some job openings, one with a furniture store as a salesperson for a few months then had to quit unexpectedly due to a hit man who came looking for me. I will get into that story in another chapter.

Then I found an ad for a live-in caregiver and got the job taking care of an elderly gentleman, who proved not to be so much of a gentleman. He was on dialysis three times a week, a diabetic, and non-believer in Jesus. I was desperate for work, so I accepted the live-in position as a caregiver. Days after I accepted the job, he moved into a larger apartment that would not accept any animals. He never mentioned to me that he had plans to move into another apartment or that he disliked dogs. I had told him of my beloved poodles I brought from California, and he didn't seem to mind or just didn't care to tell me of his dislike for them.

My two beloved poodles had to go, for animals were not allowed in that complex. My dogs seemed to know their fate, and my animals and I cried together. I loved them so very much, and they were so faithful and loyal to me all the years I had them. They were my companions during good and bad, thick and thin, through the years. To this day I regret having to give them up as I did. Years later, I had to cut the soul ties that I had developed with them. Dole seemed to have a chip on his shoulders and great dislike for people in general. He did, however, enjoy my cooking and country drives he had me take him on. You could classify him as grumpy old man who hated his life.

For one long year, I remained as Dole's housekeeper, caregiver, cook, and driver. The only time off I had was the three to four hours Dole was in dialysis three days a week and on Sunday mornings when I went to church, but I had to be home in time to fix his lunch by noon. I felt like I was a slave again even though I enjoyed doing the household routine. I just was not free but bound up with no future of my own and stuck with a man I did not like.

I tried reading the Bible to him, to no avail. He did not want to listen. He wanted to go on road trips and eat out a lot. On Sunday mornings, I was free to attend church for about three hours only. Toward the end, Dole got a little too frisky and wanted a different type of relationship—intimacy—insisting that a few hugs and kisses were nothing to be concerned about, so I should make him happy. His attitude *ended* the job immediately for me, and I left with only one hour's notice, feeling too tired and used to make excuses to him since he did not believe in the Word of God. The burden of what to do now was upon me again.

I had leased out my Bent Oak houses and was getting some rent to pay on the mortgage with nothing to spare. One lease had expired, and I moved back into one of the homes. Elizabeth and her girlfriend had lived in the other by this time but were gone again. Eventually,

I found other work. Wages were very low, especially for sales clerks, but I managed sufficiently…barely! This was not the new life I was looking for. I felt betrayed and lied to again. My escape from Egypt so far was not successful, and I was resenting it.

"Why?" was always a question I was asking God. At times, I lost all hope completely. Another disappointment. It was difficult to hope again. Even though I made a strong effort to change, without a relationship with God, there was no hope. I failed in the attempt, and it ended up just as bad as or worse than it was before. I should have known this scripture and taken it to heart:

> Now when the unclean spirit goes out of a man, it passes through waterless places seeking rest, and does not find it. Then it says, "I will return to my house from which I came," and when it comes, it finds it unoccupied, swept, and put in order. Then it goes and takes along with it seven other spirits more wicked than itself, and they go in and live there; and the last state of that man becomes worse than the first. That is the way it will also be with this evil generation. (Matthew 12:43–45 NASB)

Problems come in many different ways, shapes, and sizes. You might feel like you are making dry bricks at your place of employment, your marriage, or even with your finances, just like the Hebrews were forced as slaves to make bricks for the Egyptians. This is how I was feeling. I was worn out and hated my life. We all come across different types of problems in living out our lives. Just as God had rescued and freed the Hebrews from their problems in Egypt, He is able to free His people (those today who believe in Jesus and receive Him as their Savior and Lord) from their troubles and suffering. Jesus calls all who are burdened to come to Him in prayer, trusting in Him to set them free. I could not cry out to Him, for I was angry, confused, and disappointed. I lost faith in Him and that I could do anything good at all.

Come to Me, all who are weary and heavy-laden, and I will give you rest. Take My yoke upon you and learn from Me, for I am gentle and humble in heart, and YOU WILL FIND REST FOR YOUR SOULS. For My yoke is easy and My burden is light. (Matthew 11:28–30 NASB)

In 1989, living back in one of my Bent Oak homes, I searched diligently for a home church but was met with great difficulty. I was supposed to be in the Bible Belt—you know, the place where godly people lived. Coming from liberal California to a strict religious environment was a shock in itself. The dilemma was the religiosity in the churches. In California, women were equal to men in the ministry. Women were welcome to teach, lead, and preach, although I didn't much care for women preachers, and I surely was not called to preach. In Bent Oak, women were only allowed to teach, particularly in children's church. I had my ministerial license still active from California, but leaders only balked at me as inferior, a female, of no use or good in any ministry. Knocked down again! The ministerial license proved not to be so important to me, and I decided to just let it expire as a useless tool.

Elizabeth had quit the university because they closed down the medical school. She was attending a very tiny church led by Batty, a female pastor. I was not too impressed when I visited the church with her, but I ended up staying a few months in Batty's congregation. She was a prosperity-and-healing preacher of sorts, or so she thought. I never saw or heard of anyone actually getting healed or financially rewarded while we attended. She talked a great deal on giving and it will be given back to you.

Somehow, I got suckered into her spiel. One night I had a dream that I was to give her one of my houses lock, stock, and barrel. I had already given her all of my books and tapes from Bible college. For some reason there was still a reluctance in giving her my house too. Both houses were on the same property, which meant she would get both of them. I finally gave in, and the property was transferred to her and her husband. This proved not to be a godly decision but a deception from the adversary, Satan, again.

Almost immediately, after Batty took possession of the property, her attitude toward me changed. I could not believe my ears when one Sunday, she accused a woman in the church, whom she always referred to as Farrah Fawcett because she wore the same hair style as Farrah, as being a lesbian. She stated this woman was trying to break up a marriage between so-and-so by being good friends, delivering food and comfort to them under false pretenses. Since there were only about twelve people attending her church, most of them knew I was the Farrah Fawcett Batty was talking about, and they turned in their seats to look at me.

I was confused, still smiling, thinking this was a joke. Elizabeth had been witnessing to a young lesbian her own age in the church, and I can only surmise that Batty had evil thoughts about their relationship and me as her mother. That's when I finally woke up to the fact I had been duped (*again*), along with Elizabeth. I promptly left without making any defense to the false accusations. They already made up their minds about me and Elizabeth based on lies spoken from supposedly a godly person from the pulpit.

After securing a secular attorney, I actually got my houses back but had to pay up the past-due mortgage that Batty and her husband never paid. My books, tapes, cookware, all my antique furniture, even heirlooms from my mother and grandparents were taken by "the church," *aka* Batty and her husband from the apartment I let Elizabeth and her friend stay in while I was not there. Elizabeth was told by "the church" that I had sent them to collect all these belongings as donations, which I had not done. "Why would I ever trust or attend any church again?" became my position or motto.

Pondering why God allowed such a terrible thing to happen, I realized I was not hearing from God as I thought. I was not studying His Word. I was too busy trying to survive and make other people happy. It was just too easy for Satan to deceive me with lies. There was still so much I did not know about the spiritual world and how I was being used and manipulated by evil forces unknown to me at that time. I only knew enough to get into trouble.

I left that congregation and lost the friendships I had with the people there and continued to search for God. The adversary had taken my joy and faith in God. In many ways, the words we speak and our attitudes create the reality in which we live. I did not know I was in spiritual bondage, and I thought as if I was in control of my life, making decisions, but eventually, I ended up serving a great nothingness. Without God and without faith, you can live in denial as I did. My soul was starving, and I didn't know how to feed it to make me feel or be better. Hopelessness was all I felt.

Somehow I never heard or understood any message from any church that helped me grow up in the Lord and trust in Him. Their teachers, leaders would give me scripture to read but could not tell me what they really meant or how to apply them to my situations. Somehow, someway, I was supposed to be a Christian who is to live a godly life, making good decisions without counseling and help from the church. I just couldn't swallow this pill but ended up swallowing many prescription pills doctors would prescribe to help me in my depression and anxiety to help me get well and make good decisions according to them. It only made things worse for me. I felt like a drug addict at the time.

So when I got the houses back, I decided it might be best to repair some of the damages that had been done, rent them out, and move elsewhere. Elizabeth was enrolled in a med tech school and was planning to divorce her husband, whom she had married a few months before. She found that the school had a campus in Arlington, Texas, and was considering a move there to flee the abuse she had been experiencing. We both decided to move to Texas together, and we rented an apartment close to the school.

We didn't stay together long for I had unfinished business with my houses in Bent Oak that needed attention and resolve. Eventually, I did go back to Arlington, got my own apartment, and found work that led me to a position learning the art of picture framing, which was a very specialized field in the arts and crafts. After several months of training, I was offered a managerial position in one of the company's stores in Memphis, Tennessee. I joyously accepted! So I was on the move again in an old small broken-down car with a good motor.

CHAPTER 12

Deeper into Egypt

My next adventure was that of being sent to Memphis to manage a retail picture-frame shop that was doing poorly, not meeting the company standards or quotas. It was in the suburb of the big city. It was laid-back, quietly growing, and a nice place to have a good, thriving business. The owners had me go to other store locations along the way first. The first store was a manager in Arizona who needed a short vacation, a few days off. It went well. However, the second one, also out of state, was closed up when I arrived.

After calling the home office, they located the distracted manager, who had other personal things to do rather than man the store, which was in total disarray. He was fired via phone call. I stayed there cleaning the place up and taking inventory for several weeks, waiting for a new manager to arrive. There were not a lot of customers coming in, and those who did come in complained the store was far from meeting their expectations. Finally, a new manager was hired, and I moved on.

Arriving in Memphis a day earlier than the owner, I chose to use my time looking for an apartment and resting. The next day, the owner and I met in the parking lot of the store. We walked into the store together, and the manager, Juan, recognized the owner. He apparently realized he would be getting the axe by the look he saw on the owner's face. I watched the interaction between them nervously. Juan was a tall middle-aged man with dark hair and moustache who looked to be of a Hispanic descent.

The owner was there only to introduce me as the new manager then left me alone with this *fired* manager, who was allowed to stay on a few days or weeks until I felt acquainted with the store…then let him go at my discretion. Juan looked embarrassed and somewhat like a cat that swallowed an entire mouse whole. I was there to run the store, but my first two jobs were to take inventory and count the cash register. Needless to say, not only was the cash register short, so was the inventory. After reporting my findings to the home office, adjustments were made and sent to me to rectify the problem.

Juan was very amused that I had taken over but nervous about how he was going to deal with his "friends and clients" at this point. I kept him on for about two weeks to help redo window displays and finish existing job orders. During that time, he made every effort to accommodate me, even cleaning up the back rooms and putting everything in order. He made coffee every morning and afternoon just the way I liked it and served it to me.

He was somewhat attractive and well-built. He carried himself like someone who had authority and prestige. His clothes were expensive and pressed. He had dark, black wavy hair and black eyes, yet his skin was not dark. Within a short time, I became drawn to him, but I kept it to myself, for that was taboo to even think I could be attracted to him or what could happen between us against company policy and ethical standards.

The two weeks had gone by, and I found I could not let him go just yet, for there was still prior unfinished business to deal with, and he was very helpful, and I was enjoying this particular store. Well, after several months went by, we had our regular routine. We both got to the store early to prepare for the day.

As time went by, I would notice shortages in the cash register and would mention it to him. He would either shrug his shoulders or say, "You must have made a mistake." But I knew I did not make financial mistakes. Then I would put my own money in to make up for the loss. He took note of that, but shortages continued to happen periodically, which gave me great concern.

One of the many pleasures I had managing the store was my freedom to pray for people when they came in. One particular person was a young woman who was pregnant. She related to me that she was worried about her pregnancy, for she had previously miscarried several times, and they wanted a child very much. I was able to lay hands on her and the child in her womb and pray over them both. A few months later, she came back with good news: she had carried the child to full term and had a healthy baby. That made my day! The Lord is so good!

Another wonderful aspect was that of creating the art of framing window and showroom displays, including art contests through the local schools. It proved to increase our traffic and sales to some degree and was so rewarding for me to have the freedom to do that. I absolutely loved it. Being creative is in my DNA.

Once, a very lovely lady about my age came in to have her needlework framed, and we struck a good conversation regarding Christian fellowship and how I yearned to find a good church to attend. She invited me to join her that week in a ladies home Bible study at one of their homes, and I accepted. It turned out to be so delightful that I continued with them for about a year. Our group of ladies enjoyed each other's company, and I felt so grateful to have them as friends. They were all very helpful and attentive to one another. One particular lady called Lill took a liking to me and was so helpful to me in times of need. It turned out to be the highlight of my stay in that town.

Over a year had gone by when one day, I had a doctor's appointment, and the nurse practitioner found a lump in my breast. The mammogram deemed it necessary to perform a biopsy, and cancer was found. Juan came with me to my appointments and encouraged me to go through with the surgery. The doctor wanted to do a mastectomy, but I said, "Absolutely *not!*"

After much discussion, I agreed to have surgery to remove the lump, which turned out to be a five-millimeter tumor and caught in time, but they also did a severe removal of lymph nodes. During my absence from the store, Juan took charge again and returned to his old habits. He came several times to visit me at the hospital, and I did the unthinkable: I gave him the key to my apartment so he could wash my sheets and clean up for my return per his request. So consumed was I with the surgery and cancer, I didn't give much thought to what he may do while he was in my apartment.

I was in the hospital for several days and anxious to get back to work (or home, really). Upon my discharge, he picked me up and took me straight to the store. Juan had me just sit in a chair and watch for about four hours until I couldn't take the pain any longer, then he brought me home. I only needed a few more days of rest but came to the store to work earlier than planned out of fear of what Juan might be doing. I just didn't do much. I had been in an aerobics class at the apartment complex and decided to start up again and just go slowly until I built myself up again. Juan joined me in the class, to my surprise. The oncologist followed up with six radiation treatments, which later in life was found to be more damaging to me than good to my dismay.

Needless to say, I never fired Juan. Things got worse with him there, yet sales increased ever so slowly. I was never able to catch him stealing, but things would come up missing, especially the cash. One time, I had to get some pieces from another local store, and Juan wanted to drive me there. When we arrived, I left my purse holding *everything personal* and money in the car. It wasn't more than three to four minutes that I was in the store to see if the items were ready. When I went back to the car to get my money, Juan looked nervous and serious. My wallet with money, ID, and SS card and Drakes, my ex-husband's, personal information were missing from my bag! I yelled, "Oh! No! My wallet is gone!"

Juan made some excuse that I must have left it home or misplaced it somewhere, but I knew for sure I had it with me so I could pay for the order. I knew for sure he took it, but how in such a short time? I was afraid of him, having seen his temper. And what did he do with it? A barrage of questions and thoughts kept coming to my mind for days, weeks, months. Still, I never accused him or said anything about suspecting him. It seemed too late after all the time that I let go by, for I feared him, knowing he had connections to local Mafia as he had told me.

By this time, he was spending lots of time in my apartment, fixing meals to eat together and talking about family matters and the pain he suffered growing up in a divided family. In my confused mind, I did not want to believe he would be concerned for me and at the same time hurt me. Does he not have a conscience? What can I do to make him change for better?

He would occasionally try to fix my hair by brushing and pinning it differently or straightening out the clothes I was wearing. He loved to go shopping with me to get clothes and items for himself at whatever expense—no limit at times. I wondered where he was getting the money for all that stuff. At one point, he did state his father gave him a generous allowance every month of several thousand dollars. I questioned to myself if that was true since he was a big spender, but then, why was he stealing from me and the store?

Months had gone by before I discovered Juan was gay, as it was disclosed by a gay customer who came into the store to see him, and told me of his affair with him. Prior to this, Juan's ex-girlfriend came with pictures of her baby to get framed for free, thinking he was still the manager. They made loving gestures and kissed, so I never suspected he was gay. Another of Juan's close friends came to the store to see him. He was impeccably dressed and attractive, and he had just bought Juan a pricey vehicle as a gift. Juan was blushing and happy to see him. That's when I truly knew I was blinded and deceived again. I was in denial. I refused to fire him, thinking I could turn him around and save him by kindness and prayer, and perhaps no harm would come to me.

One fall night, there was a huge citywide benefit ball at a famous gay nightclub coming up to support HIV/AIDS. Juan invited me to go to a dance club, not mentioning any of the particulars of it, and I accepted. He went shopping with me to get just the right outfit and even had it altered to fit me perfectly...at my expense!

When I arrived on my own to the club, I heard very enticing, rhythmic music playing inside that I really enjoyed, and it drew me closer in. That's when I realized, as I suspected, that it was a gay dance hall. When I got inside, men were dancing with men and women with women. Juan had arrived earlier and spotted me. He took me around to meet his friends. Some of them were well-known business men in the city who were not open about this secret life. This actually put me in peril later on when I eventually left Memphis to return to Texas. We danced together in a group, but I refused to have any drinks since I had driven myself there and would be driving home.

At one point, I wanted a better look at this huge place, so I climbed up the stairs to the balcony. Fear gripped me as scriptures of Sodom and Gomorrah came upon me. I could not believe what men were doing to one another seated around the dance floor. Fear of God came upon me, and I ran down the stairs and made a very quick dash out of the building without saying goodbye to anyone, got in my car to safety, and drove off. The thought that fire and brimstone could hit that place made me run like a frightened chicken. Images I saw stayed with me through the years. I was relieved and grateful I had never succumbed to that kind of life. The music had drawn me and many others into that place—Lucifer at work, the deceiver!

Several of the men I was introduced to who were married with children had left or were leaving their wives and families for the gay lifestyle. The music was so enticing, but what I heard and saw was not the lifestyle I wanted or desired. How could I break Juan away from all this? How can I get away from this?

In a vision one night, I was transported from one place to another in the spirit to Juan's bedroom. Juan and his close friend were there in the room, having pleasure with one another. To this day, I believe the Lord brought this vision to me as a warning to stay away from this unhealthy life and make it clear about Juan's status. The next day, I decided to confront Juan with this, and when I told him of my *vision* and explained what I saw, he became angry and paranoid, saying I had spied on him at his house. He refused to discuss the issue, and he immediately had drapes made to cover the high windows of his bedroom. He had no understanding of spiritual matters, not even the Word of God. He did not want to hear what I had to say.

For the next two years, I fell deeper into Egypt, greater despair and bondage. I had not found a good church to attend and only went occasionally as I felt the urge to go to one nearby. I simply journaled to God for relief, hoping He was with me. My life was in turmoil. I was in despair most of the time. My journaling revealed the tortured state of mind I was in with seemingly no way out. I made journal entries almost daily. Here are a few I'm sharing to those who may be reading this book so they may know my frame of mind then and be able to relate to same issues I was facing.

February 25, 1992

> Lord, I believed I could learn from Juan, and I wish he could learn from me—something, anything. What? I had hoped my faith in God, but even that is wavering. I find myself to be fifty years old according to my driver's license, but in spirit, body, and mind, I have not arrived there yet. I feel like I am being punished for being fifty and being punished for not being fifty. What a curse it is to me. I need counseling and spiritual help so badly right now to get me through this time, but so far, God, You haven't made any spiritual counseling available to me or any good basic counseling. So what is it You propose to do for me? Help me get through this day in Jesus's name.

March 3, 1992

> Well, it's 7:30 a.m., and I've got the shakes again. I don't know if it's due to the Prozac or something else. The thought of being alone for another twelve months in this apartment is depressing. The prospect of meeting someone I care to share my apartment and life with seems pretty slim to

me right now. I'm feeling too devastated to get involved. I just need friends to go places and do things with. But I keep finding something wrong with everyone I meet and rule them out. Guess I'm really afraid of being taken and hurt over and over again. I just need to lean more on the Rock of my foundation. I'm going to get through this and be an even better, stronger person.

Sometimes I feel it's more bliss to be ignorant about certain facts of life. I hate having to grow up, but we all must sooner or later. I guess there is something to be said about being old and *wise*. Well, here I go to face the world again today. God be with me!

June 17, 1992

Now please forgive me if I'm in error, but I thought You said in Your Word that You are my covering when there is no man in my life. Your Word says, "I shall not want," that You "spread a table before me." Yes, I have food to eat, but, Lord, You are eating better than I. Is that the way a husband should treat his wife? My physical needs go unmet, and I very often fall into the trap of lusting. That is not becoming or faithful of a wife, so what is the answer?

You know that I cannot force myself lately to read Your Word every day like I used to because of my "wants and needs" (the flesh) overpowering me. I am helplessly left to Your mercy and forgiveness. As I said, there has *never, never* been any man in my life I have been able to trust or love because of their neglect, abandonment, and severe abuse. I have trouble trusting and relating to You, Father, because of that, I am sure. There's been *no* fatherly love, kindness, and nurturing, only neglect, rejection, and abuse.

When a wife is tired or ill, is it not the husband's responsibility to look after her and care for her until she's back on her feet? So why are You not taking care of me so I can get back on my feet and attend to responsibilities? If I'm in error here, please talk to me and tell me where I am going wrong, but don't shut me out. I'm not the wife in Proverbs 31, but I want to be. I need You, Husband, in order to be that wife.

Yes, I believe I could be much happier single if I at least had better finances and living conditions instead of barely making it from paycheck to paycheck. Have I not proven to You that for me, money is not the answer to everything? No, I haven't forgotten all the miracles You have done in my life, but I'm confused as to why if this is the end result. Please explain so I can understand, so I can witness it. If I could only touch the hem of Your garment.

July 9, 1992

Father, I'm sorry I've let You down so many ways. I can't recall or count them. Even now, I'm pretty sure I'm struggling with a hardened heart, unforgiveness, doubt, selfishness, apathy, and whatever else. Oh, yes, fear of man, rejection, and the unknown.

Father, in my mind, I can ask for forgiveness and even forgive to a point. But in my heart, there's an inability to get to that repentant—sorry, changed—state that I know is necessary. So I ask You to help me get there, to a repentant heart and mind to forgive everyone, including myself and You. I can't do it alone. You know me better than I know myself. My mind and body want that which I know I shouldn't have. My spirit is exhausted and tired from being hit and badgered, and I need help. Who else can I call out to help me, Father? Only You.

July 29, 1992

You know the depth of my anguish and pain, the remorse and the grief I suffer. Only You know the way out of this dilemma I have put myself in, and only You can get me out of it. Why is it I always have to be rescued out of trouble? Why can't I ever do things right? Lord, You know how very tired I am, how I look for rest soon, very soon. I can see Your point about being alone versus having to put up with a mate's demands and wishes, yet it seems some of the weight on me might be lifted or shared. On the other hand, my experience has been to carry not only my load but theirs too! Too, too much for me to bear ever again!

Even now, my desire to have another dog as a companion is quenched by the burdens I already face. It seems like too much to deal with. Yet I'd give anything for my dogs Collette and Dolly to be with me now. I miss them so much. Will I ever get over their loss, the grief? They sustained me and gave me so much. How could I have given them up? I know, I remember: a sacrifice in order to win Dole, the man I did caregiving for, over to You. It didn't work. I failed. I'm alone and grieved and angry for having let them go.

I'm sorry that I'm not a better witness and worker for You, Lord. I continually fail You, it seems. I fail my own expectations. People continually fail me. They are a great disappointment. Not only do I hurt for myself, but I hurt for them. The world is so screwed up. It saddens me. It makes me sick. It makes me run and hide, get away from them so I won't be contaminated, but of course, You know I already am stained. Fix me and make me better. Help me help myself to be a healthy, whole person, a great example, someone to be admired and sought after for the love, giving, and caring of others I should have.

I sense that Elizabeth truly needs me now, pregnant with a second child. I'm not there for her. I wish I could be without having to go through great tragedy and turmoil. Lord, please, in Jesus's name, help me through this time and make things right. Help Elizabeth and Rodney in every area of their lives and watch over their first-born continuously. Take care of Juan in whatever way You must, but spare his life and his family. Do whatever You must to protect each one.

Why can't I hear Your direction for my life? Why must I continually make the wrong decisions and suffer the consequences? Can You make it a little easier for me, Lord, please? I'm so tired of the struggle. I guess since I won't be taking a vacation now like I had planned, I'll take it all in September to be with Elizabeth when she has the baby. How disappointed I am.

At one point, I asked Elizabeth and Rodney if they wanted to come and visit me since I was renting a loft on the third floor an older building downtown. Elizabeth had their second child by then, and they came for a short vacation. Upon arrival, I grabbed the newest-born child and literally ran up the three flights of stairs with him in my arms without stopping, which blew them away since I was in my fifties and considered a senior. I kept myself in good shape by working out and walking a lot. Juan allowed them to use the pool at his home for one day, which was a godsend since the electricity gave out in the flat in the ninety-plus-degree weather we were having. Between no electricity, the very hot weather, and having to climb three flights of stairs to the loft, they went home exhausted from the trip.

Now year 2018, I see these previous years were spent in self-pity, malcontent, and complaining constantly, which was a sign of ingratitude toward God. I was undermining my own spiritual growth. The power of speech is a big deal. I was dwelling on the past and negative experiences, speaking them out of my mouth, which I was in the habit of doing. The power of the tongue can create a world of chaos around us by our negative speech. The Lord hears and sees our words. So does the devil. We are allowed to reap what we have sown, for God is our Parent who wants to correct and instruct His children. Positive thinking and speaking His Word create for us, for me, a positive atmosphere and resolve rather than a negative one, resulting in a bad attitude. But I had trouble learning this.

First Corinthians 10:9–13 (NASB) says,

> Nor let us try the Lord, as some of them did, and were destroyed by the serpents. Nor grumble, as some of them did, and were destroyed by the destroyer. Now these things happened to them as an example, and they were written for our instruction, upon whom the ends of the ages have come. Therefore let him who thinks he stands take heed that he does not fall. No temptation has overtaken you but such as is common to man; and God is faithful, who will not allow you to be tempted beyond what you are able, but with the temptation will provide the way of escape also, so that you will be able to endure it.

Love can hurt sometimes, and it can be hard at times, but love can makes a way for you to feel like you are alive and worth living while it endures.

1994 Journal

Thank You, God, for showing me I can truly love, to have feelings for someone else, that I am not numb or dead but was able to love a man—Juan. We never held hands, hugged, or had an intimate relationship, but we cared for one another for a short time—real or not, only God knows.

When it was found that I had breast cancer, he was there for me. He waited on me and wanted to be with me. When I was in the hospital, he was there. He took care of my laundry, food, needs at home, and was very attentive. Every day, he made coffee and meals exactly like I loved it and served it to me—a very small thing but big in my eyes. No one else ever was personal with me in a caring way.

When he got into an auto accident, I waited on him. At first, he didn't want me near because of open wounds. He had not yet told me about his terminal illness, HIV/AIDS. I found out much later. I cooked for him, did his laundry and ironing, helped bathe him to remove the glass pieces off his body very carefully. Obviously, it was a scary thing to think you might get AIDS/HIV for just being a friend. Much later I got tested for HIV and AIDS and was negative. It wasn't clear to me at that time just how one might contract the disease, so I actually joined an HIV group to learn of it and how to prevent contracting the disease.

We enjoyed being in the same room, crying together, having fun, laughing, and simply enjoyed each other's company during that short time. Now, I realize it was an *illusion of the deceiver* to sway me down the wrong path.

Suffering a loss so deep in my heart, I thought I could never stop the pain, the hurt, and cried deeply for days when I found out Juan's preferred lifestyle. The suffering was immense and long-lasting. I felt he had given up his life as God created it to be and turned himself over to Satan's devices. He came to church with me a few times to see if he liked *religion* or not but quit going after a few visits. I was able to lead him in a prayer of salvation, but no one knows but God whether he was sincere or not in his heart. He continued to pursue his friends in pursuit of happiness.

Finally, I realized the entire relationship had been a *lie* from start to finish. To think I was contemplating spending the rest of my life with him as a close friend boggles my mind. How could anyone be so needy? How easy it was for me to be deceived and taken down the wrong path of life. "How is this possible?" you may ask. I still had not learned to make Jesus (Yeshua in Hebrew) the Lord of my life and to keep my eyes on Him. I had not learned to put my trust in Him.

Seeing that His divine power has granted to us everything pertaining to life and godliness, through the true knowledge of Him who called us by His own glory and excellence. For by these He has granted to us His precious and magnificent promises, so that by them you may become partakers of the divine nature, having escaped the corruption that is in the world by lust. (2 Peter 1:3–4 NASB, Emotional Healing)

Depart from me, all you who do iniquity,
For the Lord has heard the voice of my weeping.
(Psalm 6:8 NASB, Fear)

July 6, 1994

Dear Lord, I am confident You are still with me, though I falter from hour to hour. Again, will You help me out of my trouble? The possibility of a *contract* on my life is ever more real than before. I've stopped being Juan's "puppy dog," and he's angry, irritated, frustrated, and the only thing he knows to do is eliminate me from his life.

Juan's friends figure I know too much about their secret lifestyle and may ruin their lives, business, and established friendships around town by me possibly speaking out and exposing the truth.

So I just have to let it go and let God do the work, the shake-up! God has used me in many mighty ways. Why should it be any different now? I am not afraid of the unknown. No one ever wants to have to suffer or be frightened to death. As long as I recognized God's presence with me at all times, I can stand.

We are afflicted in every way, but not crushed; perplexed, but not despairing; persecuted, but not forsaken; struck down, but not destroyed. (2 Corinthians 4:8–9 NASB, Discouragement)

By this time, I had decided to quit managing the frame shop and take the offer of my competitor across the street, who owned a more traditional picture frame shop. Since Juan was still working with me, he would take over my store until they found someone else to replace him. I had to get away from him. My curiosity got the best of me, wanting to see how this other store was surviving in the picture-frame business.

Right off, I didn't like the way her store was set up and her rigid rules on framing, for she did not see it as a form of art but rather strictly business, which meant she cut every corner she could, resulting in lesser quality. She had a young college man working for her, who was very talented but being held back by owner's restrictions. When the owner was not there with us in the shop, I instructed him in how to be creative without wasting a lot of expensive materials. He was thrilled, and as it turned out, when he showed his finished piece to the owner, she was delighted, and it gave him courage to use his imagination. I told him not to tell her I had helped him, and he didn't.

Unfortunately, Juan's friends would come into the store before closing to try to persuade me to go work for them and would provide housing as well. They were frightening!

Feelings of guilt and betrayal overwhelmed me for going to work for this competitor after having been trained so well and given opportunity to manage a wonderful contemporary store by previous frame shop owners. There was a strong desire to see how she was running the business, but she didn't deserve my skills. I gave notice to her after only three short weeks of working there, and I found work at a local church in their accounting department, which felt very comfortable with the experience I already had. I had no intention of letting this other store owner use my skills to promote herself and her business. She was so disgruntled at my leaving and fed up to the point she said she wanted to get out of the business, sell the place. I didn't stick around long enough to find out whether she did or not. I didn't care!

February 15, 1995

I don't trust anyone, can't believe what anyone says. Nothing spoken is ever backed up or demonstrated to be fact. I have absolutely no idea what to think or plan for tomorrow or the next day or next week, month, or year. That's so unlike me, always planning for something. Now, I'm just drifting through time and space without a path or destination or purpose.

It's so hard to smile or laugh now. I remember many times of being carefree, fun loving, sweet and kind, enthusiastic, adventurous, funny, sexy, and witty. Somehow, somewhere, I lost them all, and there's nothing to pull out, just emptiness. I can't even dream or imagine like I used to. That was a great escape for me, and I enjoyed it.

As I sit here on my bed, all I can think of is sleeping tonight and making it through another day tomorrow. Tonight, I get to be held by my Father in heaven. He is my Father, my Lover, my Husband, and I just want Him to hold me tight and rock me and love me and walk with me in His arms. I want to feel safe and secure and wanted and peaceful.

Through these years, I learned so many people are full of lies, and I believe that they live and operate by those lies knowingly or unknowingly. The world is full of lies and deception and uses those lies to promote themselves for gain, for they are deceived by the adversary, Satan. Many believe the lies they receive just as I had.

He sent from on high, He took me;
He drew me out of many waters.
He delivered me from my strong enemy,
And from those who hated me, for they were too
mighty for me.
They confronted me in the day of my calamity,
but the LORD was my stay.
He brought me forth also into a broad place;

He rescued me, because He delighted in me.
(Psalm 18:16–19 NASB, Oppression)

By this time, I was severely depressed, which is the enemy of faith, and felt I had lost the battle. Yet there was still a determination to move on. There had to be something more, something better.

My love for framing caused me to continue on my own, so I rented a ground-floor flat of a house that could accommodate the framing business and my love for painting. I loved it but did not make a dime. Then I was flooded by a heavy rain. Again, I was flooded even worse to where the immediate neighbors who knew of this place came to assist me, getting furniture and equipment up off the floor. I had subleased the flat from a businessman who knew it would flood but failed to tell me. This is when I decided it was time to return to Texas and leave without telling the sublessor for all the damage and grief it caused me. The place was a mess!

God allowed me to suffer for the choices I made choosing sin over Him and was silent to me much of the time even though I was not fully conscious that I was sinning. I fell into extreme self-pity through those years, a spiritual blindness. If only I had read and understood the true meaning of these scriptures:

> For even though they knew God, they did not honor Him as God or give thanks, but they became futile in their speculations, and their foolish heart was darkened. Professing to be wise, they became fools, and exchanged the glory of the incorruptible God for an image in the form of corruptible man and of birds and four-footed animals and crawling creatures.
>
> Therefore God gave them over in the lusts of their hearts to impurity, so that their bodies would be dishonored among them. For they exchanged the truth of God for a lie, and worshiped and served the creature rather than the Creator, who is blessed forever. Amen.

For this reason God gave them over to degrading passions; for their women exchanged the natural function for that which is unnatural, and in the same way also the men abandoned the natural function of the woman and burned in their desire toward one another, men with men committing indecent acts and receiving in their own persons the due penalty of their error.

And just as they did not see fit to acknowledge God any longer, God gave them over to a depraved mind, to do those things which are not proper, being filled with all unrighteousness, wickedness, greed, evil; full of envy, murder, strife, deceit, malice; they are gossips, slanderers, haters of God, insolent, arrogant, boastful, inventors of evil, disobedient to parents, without understanding, untrustworthy, unloving, unmerciful; and although they know the ordinance of God, that those who practice such things are worthy of death, they not only do the same, but also give hearty approval to those who practice them. (Romans 1:21–32 NASB, Unbelief and Consequences)

For sighing comes to me instead of food; my groans pour out like water. What I feared has come upon me; what I dreaded has happened to me. I have no rest, but only turmoil. (Job 3:24–26 NIV, Deficiency)

CHAPTER 13

Return to Texas

After the second flood in the last apartment I subleased in Memphis, I decided to call Elizabeth and Rodney to see if they would drive to Memphis and help me move back to Texas. They agreed and within a couple of weeks came with their two little boys in tow. Even though I got the largest U-Haul truck, we couldn't fit everything in it. We had to leave a lot of items behind, most of it ruined by water. Had the person who leased it told me the place flooded in heavy rains, I would not have leased it, of course.

Rodney drove the U-Haul truck, and Elizabeth drove their loaded station wagon with the kids and me. My vehicle packed to the full was being towed behind the truck. Feelings of failure, embarrassment, shame, inferiority, resentment, anger, sorrow were heavily on my shoulders. I did not want Elizabeth or Rodney to see how I was feeling. I stayed fairly quiet all the way back to Texas. They had no idea what I had been going through the last few years and especially the last few months. I didn't want them to know. In their minds, I was already a disgrace, a nonmother to Elizabeth, always getting into troublesome issues, needing help with them or someone else to get out of my situations. Now, I just proved and confirmed their beliefs. My heart was aching and overwhelmed with grief.

Upon arrival, they prepared a place for me to stay in their home and even fixed a small area of the garage for me to continue the business of picture framing. They were truly trying to make me feel comfortable and welcome. I thought it was wonderful and generous, but I was feeling so depressed and burned out. The last thing I wanted to do was picture framing at that moment.

Unfortunately for me, I was not able to express my sadness, embarrassment, and shame into words. Not communicating my feelings verbally and slow responses to questions in conversations with Elizabeth seem to upset her all the more. My silence did not go well with her either. She was quick to respond and process information, but my lack of conversation made her think I was disappointed in her, her marriage, her home, and her lifestyle. Some of that was actually true, although I never came right out and stated it. I was too depressed and oppressed by the devil's tormenting lies, but no one could see it, or if they did, they didn't want or didn't know how to help me. I could not find a way to dig myself out.

Needless to say, my stay with them was short for a mother or mother-in-law live-in, for it was not an ideal living situation for them or for me at that time. My solution to everything was to leave, get up and get out, move away, another job, or another people group. I was unable to cope with or fix relationships and situations. My endless quest for help went unheard or misunderstood by churches, doctors, Christian and non-Christian organizations, even my own family. I did not know what would or even could make me better, but all those people thought they had the solution. Pastors and some Christians threw scriptures at me with no explanation or understanding.

Doctors would give me mind-controlling drugs, which made my thinking and actions worse. One doctor sent me to a hypnotist who fell asleep while trying to hypnotize me. There were minutes of silence then his snoring began until he woke himself up. I had to pay him too for the time he slept. It did not work for me!

Non-Christian and other secular group programs put me through twelve-step sessions that never solved anything. No one could or would tell me how to fix myself. It only made me more frustrated. At times, I just wanted to scream or cry without stopping.

Over the next few years, I went back and forth to Bent Oak to repair my homes and live in them. While I was there, I acquired two newborn female feral cats, which helped me survive through many difficult times. They were like good medicine, and I loved them dearly.

One time before I got the cats, Elizabeth and Rodney moved to another home where I ended up staying for a while again in Texas. I had set up my office and makeshift bed in my large van and would do my work on the computer, at times microwaving food to eat and at times sleeping in the van parked in front of their new home. I wanted to be independent and be in a quieter place to live and work than with all the children's noise and chaos. I had a need to be independent and responsible for myself. I felt and was homeless and cold, for it was winter.

When I finally repaired and sold my Bent Oak homes, I purchased a home on a double lot in Fort Worth, finding work nearby. I really loved it for its English Tudor charm and especially the empty lot next to the house, which I also purchased. I turned it into a park-like setting, enjoying every moment digging dirt and planting flowers and plants. It was the best therapy for me I had found beside my cats. The neighbors favored the new cleaned-up lot as well and were amazed that I did it alone.

Since I kept getting sick or losing jobs, I fell behind on my mortgage payments and gave in to renting out a room to a couple. It did not go well, forcing me to sell the home. I loved that home more than any other place I have lived. The floors were all hardwood, except the one and only bathroom, which Rodney completely updated, putting in new tile in shower-bath.

The home had a separate dining room with an old-fashioned stand-alone gas heater against the wall, which basically warmed the entire house. The kitchen was very large and begging for renovation. I could have made it into a large kitchen area with a good-size breakfast nook and even a laundry room at the very back. The back door had an old-fashioned screened wood door that would slam shut upon entering or leaving the house. I got very attached to that slamming screen door, for it reminded me of being in the country. There was an oversized old two-car garage in the back that would have made a great workshop with an apartment over it. It never came to pass. It was a beautiful place in my eyes with so much potential. I grieved having to leave it. The home was sold, and the beautifully landscaped yard and lot were again transformed into a less-desirable state by the new owners.

From there, I bought a used mobile home and set it on an acre in Beshua way out of town. Still changing and losing jobs, I was forced to move out and rent it out as well. After about a year, the renters disappeared without notice, and the mobile home was eventually repossessed after it sat empty for another year.

But while I lived in my mobile home, there were ground flood issues due to the land not being properly prepared. Some of the land was eroding, sliding out from under the homes that had been placed on piers or bricks, making it dangerous in the rainy seasons. My one-acre plot was next to a man-made drainage creek that started to erode away, allowing water to flood into the back half of the acre.

We, the residents, were angry enough that I volunteered to write a letter of complaint to proper authorities, along with a signed petition from the neighbors, even sending a letter to the state government. Nothing ever improved while I was there. I watched as mobile homes were being repossessed and animals left behind in total confusion. It broke my heart to see the animals suffer so. What could have been a beautiful, successful community started to fall apart and decay into empty debris-filled lots.

In 2002, I ended up in the hospital with a breakdown for three days then was sent home to recuperate. Unable to work for two more weeks, I quit my job as a traveling life insurance agent and later found work again doing odd jobs such as a mobile home salesperson, stockyard vendor, assembly line, live-in caregiver, bookkeeper, and more. Because I did not have a degree, I was not considered for higher-paying jobs even though I could do a better job than someone straight out of college. That did not matter to employers. They wanted that piece of paper showing you spent time learning the way of the world in college and now deeply in debt with a student loan. Perhaps that is the way of guaranteed long-term employment to employers nowadays. The world's motto in this day and age seems to be, "If it's broken, don't fix it. Replace it."

> Not that we are adequate in ourselves to consider anything as coming from ourselves, but our adequacy is from God. (2 Corinthians 3:5 NASB, Failure)

Up to this point, I had believed all the lies the devil was throwing at me from pastors, employers, coworkers, friends, organizations, etc. My thought was they should know everything better than I. They're professionals. Lies kept me moving and searching. Restlessness overwhelmed me to find truth, a better way, more money, more of this or that, maybe even happiness.

In the summer of 2004, I was attending a nondenominational church in Fort Worth that had started a new program open to all who were interested in attending. They used a book written by John Eldredge entitled *The Sacred Romance*, which we journeyed through for several weeks, and we shared testimonies with one another of our past and present journeys. I found it to be very prophetic and enlightening to me. There was a moment or time of abiding resignation for me, having left something behind as I stood in another crossroad of time. I wrote,

> The fantasy of Christmas lost in religion, violent and intimidating family circles, peer pressure and emptiness of life and bread on the table. In small stolen, void moments, I can see, smell, and feel it beckoning me to come, only to have it shattered like millions of pieces of broken glass at the sound and breath of those who mock because they have not seen nor heard the wildness of their own heart. My joy may be stolen for a moment, but deep inside, my heart leaps with grand and exciting expectation that my longings are being met and prepared as I walk along the avenues of

life. The next corner perhaps, will be the vision,
will be Christmas forever.

Finally, feeling like I was growing up, I had to leave behind the
fantasies in my mind, the lies that I believed and had grown to expect
and want.

We were asked to recall our best memories from childhood,
recapturing sights and sounds, the aromas and our feelings at the
time, which brought me back to a pleasant memory. I wrote,

> Early summer living with my grandparents riding
> in back of their big turquoise Packard, with a big
> silver bird glued to the cars nose, into the coun-
> tryside of Gilroy, California, to pick up a twen-
> ty-gallon flask of red wine. We always stopped at
> the same bakery for fresh Italian bread, sweet to
> the taste, crunchy on the outside and oh, so soft
> inside, still warm from the oven.
>
> We'd drive just a little farther and park
> under a big shade tree, sometimes at the vine-
> yard. Then Noni would bring out the cheese and
> slice it and serve it with the warm bread. Even
> though I was very young, they still gave me wine
> to chase down the bread and cheese. It was a little
> sweet and flowed down my throat so easily.
>
> After we had our tour of their friend's win-
> ery and loaded the wine, we headed back for
> home but not before I got to pick grapes off the
> vines and eat them.
>
> The moment we started driving back, I
> would fall asleep. I loved the sights and smells of
> the country, even the quietness and gentleness of
> it. It was always colorful, beautiful, and so very
> peaceful. That was one place I didn't hear people
> yelling or arguing. It was silent, except for the

birds and animals calling to one another and the wind dancing through the leaves of the trees.

So grateful am I that I have a good memory of living with my grandparents in my early years. I can still smell and taste the cheese, bread, and wine and remember the peace and quiet of the country. These are treasures.

We were asked in our class to write the ending of our life story the way we would like it to be, using our imagination. Within moments of picking up my pen and beginning to write, the presence of the Holy Spirit took over and was writing with my hand:

> Summer is drawing to an end. Unusual and varying as it was, it marks the end of a long journey through the open road most have traveled with their familiar identities. There's a fork in the road once again, and this time, my heart races uncontrollably with anticipation of venturing along this mysterious, exotic, less-known path, never knowing from one moment to the next what might be lurking around the next bend. Yet there's no turning back, and the road beckoning me with lesser wild lovers—a sure guarantee in this world—has grown cold and boring.
>
> As I begin my truest adventure, I am rewarded with a real estate license, opening the door to MLS and more. I don't have to look far before the Lord puts before my path a Garden of Eden clothed in various shades of brilliant greens and textures and shapes of vegetation. Forms of rock and rich earth are backdrops for the most beautiful, peaceful blue-green cascades of water that beckon you to come taste and feel and meditate in His goodness.
>
> As you walk along this new path of life, you are greeted by passionate deep forms of color

that expel the fragrance of the rose of Sharon. Entrapped by this beauty, you find other beautiful people drawn by the haunting, enjoying the wildness of this lover along with you.

Homes of imagination and grit have been built here and there, schools, dining hall, recreation center, and campsites all strategically placed for the enjoyment and living in this Garden of Eden only seen by those who dare to go after this wild lover. My home is not a mansion but rather a large bungalow with some resemblance of the Old World, planted among exotic flowers and plants in vivid passionate colors of foliage and beautiful shade trees.

There in this park, you are romanced and brought to a higher level of knowledge in the spirit and made to withstand every evil force that Lucifer and his ghouls could throw toward you. Your brightly colored armor deflects every arrow and causes it to ricochet back to its owner. This park, this Garden of Eden, invites you to eat the organic food of the promised land. Your labor is sweet and light. Just as you long for the night, so you long for the morning to come that you may dance His holy dance once again.

Look! In the distance, one is coming with the appearance of Jesus. Could that be Him? Or perhaps that's the chosen one He has selected for me to dance with here in this garden for a time. He comes as a knight on a white horse dressed in linen and silk, brilliant white hair, and eyes that pierce through the soul. His lips are ruby, and His face is ruddy. His hands are strong and sure as he lifts me onto His horse.

Though the time is short I'm allowed to experience true *phileo* and *agape* in unreserved form with this god-man, this passionate warrior of peace. Together, we comb the nations and tame the tongues of all who long to embrace something greater than their earthly plight. After some time, many are won and now know the haunting of Christ.

For a time and season, I stayed with this congregation, enjoying and growing in the Lord with them. Having lived in an apartment in Fort Worth for a year or more, I found work as an insurance adjuster and was assigned work in South Texas, which meant having to move again and find a new home for my cats, for they could not come with me. Giving up my beloved cats was extremely difficult and caused me grief I really didn't need.

After a short time in insurance adjusting, I had to give it up due to the partner agent who came with me, and I drove to Florida to meet Rodney, who also became an insurance adjuster to work for a short time with him, then we came back to Fort Worth. Then I moved into a home with a retired missionary woman five years older than myself. She had been all over the world with her husband until he passed away. We both loved the Lord and enjoyed each other's company while giving each other space and alone time. She was the best roommate I ever had.

After a year with her, she sold her home to move closer to her relatives up north. I moved into another apartment and stayed for about two years while working in real estate. Several years had passed by this time, and I was adjusting to a somewhat calmer lifestyle and work routine. I stayed in real estate, which I loved, for about eight years and eventually bought farm property that all of us, Elizabeth and her family, could live on together.

But before I recount my further wanderings, we need to go back to when I was in Bento Oak, temporarily working as a salesperson in a furniture store and the terror that took place there in my next chapter.

CHAPTER 14

The Hit Man

When I came back from Memphis in 1996 and during my short livelihood in Oklahoma, I found employment as a salesperson (one of my jobs as I previously mentioned) in a furniture store on commission only. I was living in one of my properties in Bent Oak while the other was rented out.

About three weeks after I started working, a man came into the store to inquire of me, for he had asked for me by name to assist him. He looked to be around late fifties in age, casually dressed. My boss sent me over to him. He introduced himself by first name only and said he was looking for a few things just having moved to Bent Oak. A very short conversation ensued. He asked me to lunch right then, saying he had some important information for me about my father. For some reason, he made me nervous, and it didn't feel right in my spirit to accept his invitation. He said he would be buying something for his home from me and said it wouldn't hurt to have lunch with him.

So I went to the store manager, my boss, and explained what had just transpired. He agreed for me to go with him in hopes he would really buy some furniture. I told the manager to get a good look at him in case something happens where I didn't come back. Fear was in

129

me, but just what did he know about my deceased, estranged father? Why did he come looking for me?

My boss said, "Go. Don't worry about it." So I went, hoping it was a brief lunch.

This stranger told me things I already knew about my father and some things I did not know about him. He claimed they were in the military together. He said just enough to entice me to go to dinner with him the next evening. There was something about him that caused me to distrust him, a frightening feeling, but I wanted to hear what information he had on my father, whom I did not know well and who had passed away years ago. Here I am again, believing lies of the devil.

Still thinking he may buy some furniture from me, I accepted his invitation and made arrangements to meet him at the store after work, evening time. He showed up and very briskly led me off, holding me by my upper arm. I thought that was strange. By this time, it was dark outside. Instead of taking me to a restaurant, he drove to a hotel where he was staying. I was silent and trying to figure out what he might have in his mind to do.

When he finished parking toward the back of the lot, he got out of the car and opened up the back door to his car to take out a short-looking rifle wrapped in a cloth case. My spirit said I was in trouble. This is not good! While holding the rifle or gun in one hand, he grabbed my arm and was literally pulling and pushing me in the direction he wanted to me go and not being very gentle about it either, saying he had to stop here at his room for something.

My mind and heart kept racing wildly, wondering what was about to happen. Instead of going in the front entrance, he directed me around to a back door of a hall that was unlocked. All the while, he kept looking around to see if anyone was around or watching. There was no one to be seen anywhere. He seemed nervous and in a hurry. The thought of dying was reeling in my head now. I was scared to death and gasping for air as quietly as I could, still staying silent. *How do I get out of this one? Who sent this guy? Why did someone go to the trouble of investigating me? Who hired him to dispose of me?* were my thoughts. I knew I should not anger this man.

My mind raced over my past, recalling people who were very upset with me for one reason or another. *Who needed me to be dead?* My first thought was Juan and then his friends, someone who may have been connected to the gay Mafia Juan told me about. Perhaps they thought I would blow their cover, or maybe Juan wanted revenge.

Then I thought about the Asians in California who may have finally tracked me down for having ducked out on them with the urea information I no longer had, or was it the pastor's friend in the large congregation who wanted the urea information he thought I had? Was it the Memphis guy I subleased the apartment from who never told me the place flooded and has become angered because I left and broke the lease? Perhaps it's my ex-husband, who planned my murder before I escaped and then divorced him. *Who wants me dead?* I was bombarded with various thoughts.

Should I scream for help? What about running away? There's no one around, no one to hear me, no one to see me. I was like a lamb being taken to the slaughterhouse and not being able to release itself. I stayed calm and believed God would surely help me. I can do this. Parts of various scriptures came to mind of how the Lord hears our cries and comes to rescue us, but will He really save a wretched person like me?

Finally, he opened the door to his room, pushing me in and telling me to *sit*. He put the weapon down against a piece of furniture without taking it out of the case. On the dresser, there were bottles of booze that had been opened already. He quickly got a couple of glasses and poured some kind of liquor into each glass. Handing me one, he said, "Drink!"

I took a sip without saying anything, cold chills running down my back yet sweating profusely. He swallowed his with one gulp and refilled his glass. He started talking gibberish about something. I did not understand or have knowledge of what he was saying, all the while telling me to drink. He chugged drink after drink. I kept pretending to refill my glass but only took tiny sips standing up as close to the wall as possible, still wondering who hired this *hit man* to dispose of me.

It seemed like every moment was a lifetime. He got up from the bed he had lain down on and grabbed my arm and pulled me over to the bed. I braced myself, sure I was going to be raped. How gruesome it was to think he would do that to me before killing me. He managed to get me down on the bed, and I suddenly broke my silence, and I said, "I'm sorry. I can't do this. I am in love with Juan," without thinking what I should say.

He stopped and let go of me, took another drink, and passed out on the bed. I was motionless for seconds then got up very slowly from the bed and just stood there numb, looking at him. I waited a few minutes to make sure he was really out. Quietly and slowly, I made my way to the door. As silently as I could, I unlocked the door, went out, and shut it. I ran as fast as I could with my heart racing wildly away from the hotel.

To this day, I don't remember how I got home. I knew God had saved me again! I never reported it to the cops or hotel office because they would never believe me. No one ever does! I felt they would come up with some excuse to be on the perpetrators side, so why bother? *Again, I believed the lies of the devil.*

Yes, of course, I did make it home and never saw or heard from the stranger again. Still determined to make a better life for myself, I worked on repairing my two homes so I could sell them and move away. Same old story. I found myself having to get away back to my daughter's house again. I never found out who sent this stranger (hit man) or the reason he was sent, although it was clear in my head it was for evil. The Lord knows, and I am not to give it another thought, for He is in control and intercedes on my behalf. Yet a few times through the years, I wondered about it. Everyone's sins will be exposed and judged on earth for all to hear in the near future come Judgment Day.

> The Lord is my light and my salvation; whom shall I fear?
> The Lord is the defense of my life; whom shall I dread? (Psalm 27:1 NASB, Fear)

Then they cried to the Lord in their trouble, and He brought them out of their distresses. He caused the storm to be still, so that the waves of the sea were hushed. (Psalm 107:28–29 NASB, Turmoil and Confusion)

Indeed, in our hearts we felt the sentence of death. But this happened that we might not rely on ourselves but on God, who raises the dead. He has delivered us from such deadly peril, and he will deliver us. (2 Corinthians 1:9–10 NASB, Trust)

CHAPTER 15

More Wanderings

round 2003, while I was working as a licensed real estate agent with a local broker in Fort Worth, I decided to try a very different church congregation that met on Saturdays. It was a Messianic Jewish congregation that I was not familiar with. The services were unlike any other church I had been to. They had a large cabinet at the head of the altar with a handwritten scroll inside. It would be taken out at a specific time in the service and carried up and down the aisles for everyone to see and touch. They said it was the Torah scroll, God's teachings to His people Israel (and for the Gentiles as well) written and spoken two to three thousand years ago.

The Torah is technically the first five books of the Bible. My thought was, *Why is God just now revealing this to us and to me?* Later, I found that this teaching has been around for years in Jewish and Messianic Jewish congregations around the world. I spent a total of four years in Bible theology classes and never heard of Yeshua, the Messiah.

I started attending regularly while still going to my Sunday non-denominational church, learning more about our Messiah throughout the following years. I learned that there were several Messianic Jewish congregations throughout the DFW area, all administering in slightly different ways but with same basic truths, some adhering more to Jewish traditions than others.

After attending services on both Saturday and Sunday with no days off to rest for one full year, I got worn out and had to make a decision to quit either Saturday or Sunday services. Since the Bible made it very clear to me by now that the Sabbath was given to us as the day of rest and worship to the Lord, I quit going to the Christian Sunday Services, for I was learning much more about our God and Yeshua (Jesus) on Sabbath services.

I stayed with this congregation and leader for over ten years. Again, I got involved with church finances: counting and depositing the tithes, establishing a church budget, and paying off new and very old bills, along with monthly staff reports and meetings. I worked closely with the leader, who usually did not agree with "my way" of doing things, nor did I agree with his ideas, but then he was the boss, and I was merely a volunteer, so I surrendered to his way of operations.

During those ten-plus years, there was controversy and discord as I had found in other congregations I had attended in the past. I thought it was normal but hated it. Of all places I thought there should be peace and harmony, joy and happiness, it would be the church. During my life, I had visited many denominations and non-denominational churches and found division and problems in all of them, to my disappointment.

There was a big emphasis in this assembly on being Jewish, which drove me to get my DNA done. I found I had very little Jewish blood in me, and when it was revealed to the leader, the finance position I held was given over to a *true* Jewish person. The feeling of being less than a perfect human being and unwanted hit me again and in a place I would not expect to be rejected. True Jewishness was preferred.

Several years after having worked there and having discussions on matters pertaining to church operations with the leader and not getting anywhere, I found and read a book entitled *The Bait of Satan* by John Bevere and decided to purchase another copy and give it to the leader to read. My thinking was he would see himself and his congregation in this book as I saw myself in it and hopefully make the needed changes for everyone's sake. However, after a month or two of waiting for changes and not seeing any, I decided to make an appointment with the leader and his wife at their home to discuss what I found in the book. This was to no avail, for he had not read nor intended to read the book. Who was I anyway but a lowly discharged layperson trying to disclose to the leader the error of his way (as I saw it) and how it would benefit *his* ministry and congregation to improve or change the way things were being done to grow deeper in the Lord and His Word.

Months before this took place, the Lord gave me a vision to write down for the leader and staff members...of crossing over a very deep and wide gorge on a very narrow swaying wood-and-rope bridge to move to higher ground and what God had waiting for them on the other side. They were at a crossroad, not knowing what to do at that time. It would take faith, courage, and stamina to cross that high bridge to the waiting Lord and all the blessings He had in store for this congregation and the leaders on the other side.

Well, some of the staff acknowledged the vision coming from the Lord, while the others, including the leader, thought it was ridiculous, risky, and foolish and refused to step out. They preferred to stay in their comfort zone.

Needless to say, I gave one hundred percent of myself, and it was not good enough. I lost all hope for the leader and congregation, especially after my meeting with the leader and his wife. I decided it was better for me to leave than to cause strife and more problems for them and the other members as soon as the Hebrew class that I was attending ended.

The last two months before I decided to leave the congregation, there was a huge misunderstanding between myself and the leader, for he seemed to have the impression I was personally interested in him, wanting him to leave his lovely wife. He came up to me one day, gently taking my hand in his and explaining he couldn't leave his wife, for she was so sweet. I was shocked, speechless, and confused. What did I say or do to make him even think such a thought? I had no interest in him other than helping him with his ministry to grow the church.

Shortly after that revelation, I left. I decided I didn't need *any* church after all. This was final confirmation that I needed to leave religious environments. I did not discuss the matter at all with him, for I was taken aback and confused, wondering where I went wrong. I took it as an offense, for I was still growing in the Word and did not know how to handle the situation, except by leaving. There was no discussion of the matter to him or anyone, except a brief mention of it to my daughter.

I've learned trying to defend myself only makes things worse. Yes, we do need to stand up for our beliefs as God's treasured children, but defending "our rights" only fuels fire of offense and does not bring true peace.

These scriptures come to mind now as I look back:

> Do not destroy him, for who can stretch out his hand against the Lord's anointed and be without guilt? (1 Samuel 26:9 NASB)

> But the wisdom from above is first pure, then peaceable, gentle, reasonable, full of mercy and good fruits, unwavering, without hypocrisy. And the seed whose fruit is righteousness is sown in peace by those who make peace. (James 3:17 NASB)

In this congregation, there was an older lady my age named Becca, who was always cordial to everyone when they came in the service but usually sat alone. After a couple of years from when I first began attending this congregation, I decided to befriend her and sit next to her. I felt sorry for her and would have casual conversation with her.

As the years went by, the communication between us turned to life's disappointments and complaints we both had about life while I was attending there. It was not edifying but rather releasing anguish, suffering, and dismay to one another, confirming our dissatisfaction in life to one another.

By this time, I had I purchased a four-and-a-half-acre farm in 2010 for myself and family (Elizabeth, Rodney, and their children). The house was a small two-bedroom, two-bath home, a very tight squeeze. I ended up having to purchase an RV to live in while the family lived in the house. My RV was parked right outside the front door of the home, making privacy scarce for me and the family. There was much tension and disagreements between me and the family and particularly Elizabeth and Rodney. The living situation was just not working out between us, so after five years and three different broken-down RVs, I decided to get out. I sold the last RV to have finances to find somewhere else to live. It was going to be difficult, as I presumed, because my only income was Social Security. The jobs I had ended when I took a bad fall on the farm and severely sprained my ankle and was unable to get around for a couple of months before I left the farm.

When I bought the property, there was a government credit or rebate of a few thousand dollars, which I took, and I went on an archaeological tour of Israel with an out-of-state Messianic Jewish organization that first year we moved onto the property. There was a lot of prestudying I had to do before we embarked, but I loved the study of the land and how it correlated with the Bible.

At the end of the two-week trip, I did not want to go back home to the US, for there was a spiritual presence there that I never felt anywhere else I have traveled to. I cried. To experience the land Jesus (Yeshua) lived and walked on, to breathe the same air, to drink the same incredibly good water, to cross over the sea He walked on, to feel the dirt that grew the food the apostles and He ate were life-changing for me. I wanted more of Him. I wanted to stay in His homeland. I was so lifted up and full of Yeshua upon returning. I couldn't handle or bear any opposition with anyone, but there was mostly with my family. Depression came over me when I returned to the farm, but I did stay those five years on the farm, trying to work it out with them. We just didn't see eye to eye on much of anything (there was an evil force over us, causing division, but we were not aware of it).

Now my friend Becca, who was attending that congregation, was in an abusive marriage, and she called me to help her escape. My grandson and I helped her move out of her home while her husband was there, fussing and cussing about the move. We could not take her in our home with us, for I had no place to stay myself, and the farmhouse was already too small for the family. She ended up at a woman's shelter for two months then went to live with a member of the same church we were attending.

Becca knew I was looking for a place to live and stated we could find a place to live together. For almost a year, we looked around the state of Texas, on my dime, which should have been a clue for me! We never took the time to discuss anything in depth to really know one another. That was another very big mistake that I didn't realize at the time. When I left the farm around 2015, I moved from one place to another, staying with friends who said they wanted me to come and help them out for a while or just keep them company. Becca kept in touch with me throughout these times.

One of my other friends, Laura, had a large home on acreage not too far out of town, where I stayed a couple of months, keeping her company. She and her husband had a large barn with a small apartment in it, which they rented out to a mutual friend, Mandy, we knew from the church we had all been attending years earlier, where we took classes in a Community Emergency Response Team (CERT) program and also amateur ham radio licensing. Those courses proved to be very enlightening for us.

Mandy wore her heart on her sleeve most of the time, so the saying goes. She took in stray animals, even baby squirrels that had fallen out of the trees to nurse them back to health. At one point, Mandy moved to Florida to marry her long-distance boyfriend and asked me to stay in her apartment to care for all her animals for a while. Of course I did!

During the months I visited with Laura, I moved into the cute little apartment and walked Mandy's dog and cared for her cats. Finally, I realized after a few weeks that it might be a few more months before she came back to get her belongings and her pets. I had gotten a call from yet another friend, Donna, who had moved north to Bowie, Texas. She and her husband, Bob, had purchased a home up there to retire in a much-laid-back, small-town atmosphere. Bob was disabled and very weak, not able to do much but still walking. Eventually, he became wheelchair bound. They had a small dog that was extremely hyper. Donna asked if I could please come and help her out with Bob and her dog. So I left Mandy's animals in the care of our friend Laura and wandered up north, staying with them, and found a care-giving job for a while as I watched over her dog and Bob.

While staying there, I was still looking for a place for Becca and me to live. Becca came and stayed with us in Bowie a couple of days, but she hated the area and the people. Donna and Bob immediately discerned Becca's spirit, and they wanted her to leave from their home. Becca left promptly but still called me to find a place for the two of us to live together. I wonder how I did not pick up on Becca's character even then. I was in denial and refused to look at our issues square in the face.

So from Bowie after I completed my stay with Donna and Bob, I started driving north and east with Becca to Gainesville, Sherman, Paris; down to Mount Pleasant, Tyler, Jacksonville; and west toward Fort Worth again. Becca was with me on some of these routes and did not like any place I drove to when we got there, so we decided to head west toward Jacksboro, Graham, Breckenridge, down to Eastland, then Ranger, where I found a great one-bedroom house I alone could afford. Had Becca not been with me, I would have tried to rent that place.

Becca wanted to go back to Alaska or farther northwest on the very top of a high mountain—in Texas? She got tired of looking and went back to where she was staying. I kept up the search. By now, you would think I would have realized it was never going to work living with Becca, but apparently, I was blindsighted and still not asking and praying to the Lord about what I should or should not do with her.

When I finally did find a place way out of town in the rural countryside of Dublin, she moved in with me, not having seen the location or house. It was a two-bedroom, one-bath house in the middle of pastures and farmland—no neighbors or any close stores, only cows now and then grazing nearby, and very quiet, which I loved. The road was dirt and rock for about a mile to the house.

She was aghast and did not want to pay for anything nor help to do anything. The brand-new refrigerator I purchased on my own dime was filled with her food, leaving no space for me at all. She very emphatically said she hated the furniture I bought for us to use in that place. The relationship got so bad, I went out into the sandy yard and cried out to God, pouring sand and dirt over my head and ripping my shirt, remembering the agony of Mordecai in the book of Esther in the Bible when the Jews were about to be slaughtered. Why was this happening to me? Why must I suffer so in this life?

Grief overtook me again. "My God Adonai, what should I do? Help me!" I cried with now-muddy tears. I had believed the rented house was a gift from God for us to stay and enjoy life even though there was no Jewish Messianic congregation anywhere near to attend. Now I could understand the frustration she had in her marriage, and why it ended in a divorce.

By the end of the month, Becca moved back into the city where she had been staying without ever paying her share of expenses. Fortunately, I was able to get out of the lease, for the owner refused to do any repairs that were badly needed.

Meanwhile, I had contacted Bear, a gentleman in his eighties Becca mentioned, who had been attending the "same congregation," to see if he knew of any place I could afford to move to since he was supposed to be in real estate. Conversing on the phone, he stated he owned a twenty-five-plus-acre parcel of land in the neighboring town, about one hour away from where I was staying. He said he had a place I could afford to move into for free, but the specifics of the place were not mentioned, nor did I ask. I just trusted his word. He said he was working on turning his property into a place of refuge, a haven for retired vets and senior women to finish out their years. Wow! I embraced the wonderful idea, and he and his sons came and moved me to *his* property. I was in disbelief. How could this happen?

How naive, stupid, and trusting I was even in my old age and after all that I had been through to believe a want to be Christian in the church. Apparently, I had no discernment when it came to my own affairs. I was duped again! Prior to my surprise on arrival, I was so excited to help this man with his praiseworthy project. The Lord had answered my prayers, or so I thought!

When we arrived, the place he had in mind for me was his back bedroom! *Red flag!* The entire house was all torn up, missing walls and ceilings. This particular bedroom had a bathroom attached but in poor condition. The wall between the two back bedrooms was missing, and the carpet of the next room was growing mushrooms! There was a hole in the bedroom roof, allowing rain to pour into the rooms. The smell was awful.

I realized I was trapped for the moment and decided to make the best of it. Was this the answer to my prayers? Did God send me here to help this poor old man, or was this another trap of the enemy? He was dying of cancer (he said) but still had strength to drive a huge commercial lawn mower of sorts and other farm equipment. He was on heart medication as well, he later confessed.

The first day of arrival, the kitchen was in total disarray. You could not see the counter or sink for all the dirty dishes, pots, pans, etc. lying around, and the smell of the old dirty dishes and slime was so bad, I could hardly keep from vomiting. However, I decided to clean everything up myself. It took hours to clean up that entire section of the kitchen. That's when I discovered he had no electricity in the kitchen, no way to cook. The refrigerator had cords strung over to it from another room to keep it running. When I opened the refrigerator door, the odor almost knocked me over, and I quickly slammed it shut! I already had enough fussing with the smelly dishes pots and pans…and now the green and black mold?

In that first week, I tackled the bathroom and bedroom carpet that was growing mushrooms. Bear helped me move the carpet bit by bit and carry it outside. Next was removing all the floor staples so feet would not get torn up. My knees got more roughed up then than any prayer time I ever spent down on all fours. After several floor washings, it didn't look or smell so bad.

After various calls I made for free installation of electric in the kitchen for this "poor vet," a company came out and did all the work in a matter of hours for free. Bear was so elated, and so was I. Now I could cook a meal.

He said he wanted to bring in more senior women to live there. Becca had called me to see if she could come join us, and she did one month later *after* the place was cleaned up as much as possible. I decided to help more by contributing to the cause of a refuge for women, so I went shopping for him. I purchased two single beds and linens and decorated the room for women to stay, cleaned up the bathroom, and got new furnishings for everything at my expense. I was not happy about Becca coming, but that was her and Bear's decision.

A few weeks later, Bear's girlfriend, who did not know Becca and I were there, came. Bear had not told her anything. All hell broke loose when she arrived, finding us living there, and she demanded we leave immediately, cursing at us even though Becca had arrived with an expensive very large, newer RV she had purchased and was parked away from the main house, hoping to stay there for free. I stayed silent and prayerful. Bear argued with his girlfriend that he wanted us to stay and help him. There was a lot of tension between people living there and those who came to visit. So much for peace and tranquility! She did not appreciate anything I had done and thought I was pursuing her boyfriend, Bear.

I had become so joyful up until then that the Lord had chosen me to help this old man with home improvements and his vision. It made me feel so special to God that He would appoint me on this endeavor, that I could possible make a difference to anyone and actually do physical labor in my old age.

By this time, Bear's son said he owned the small RV on the property and would sell it to me, that I could pay it out in monthly payments then would transfer the title over to me when it was paid in full. When I had paid 1,500 dollars, half of the cost of what he was asking, I found out he didn't have a title on it or that he even owned it. Later, he confessed it belonged to someone else who had a loan on it from the bank and told me when the loan was paid off, he could get the title. *Duped again!*

I never got my money back, nor did I seek revenge or hostility, for I was never given receipts for any payments I made, nor did I ever ask for any. I just trusted his word. Instead, I asked the Lord to reveal his folly to him and forgive him for the evil perpetrated on me. Yes, I was very angry, but I had to let it go, give it to the Lord to resolve, or I would end up suffering for lack of forgiveness. I truly enjoyed living in the small RV outside of Bear's house for that short time.

Bear had a huge barn full of used goods from house wares to building supplies and auto parts. He said he wanted to sell everything to have cash for property improvements. It all had to be tagged and priced after cleaning and reorganizing, and I volunteered to do it…alone. No one else wanted to be involved, not even his own family. Bear's rabbi friend Ralph came over weekly for prayers and Bible study and volunteered to help with the barn. Once we got it all ready to sell after advertising in the local newspaper, Bear changed his mind and refused to part with any of it. He wanted to keep the memories, he said. We had to turn away the prospective buyers who got upset driving that far out of town for nothing.

Meantime, the well's water pump broke, and we had no water for over three weeks. Becca and I had to haul water in on our own, for Bear said he was not supposed to drive. We drove into town to the YMCA for showers and to his son's property to haul water back to Bear. A group of veterans heard about the water problem and came to repair the pump at their cost for Bear's sake.

This is when Bear suddenly had a change of heart about those living on the property with him. He became a threat to us living there, as well as the rabbi. Bear had even confronted the plumbers I called for free plumbing repairs one day, for when they arrived, he started telling them he was a *murderer* and "killed people," scaring them. They turned around and left in haste, looking at me as though I had put them in danger by some crazy man. I was flabbergasted and did not know what to say or do. I just watched them hurriedly walk away while Bear was smiling and insulting them.

During the water crisis and barn episode, Bear spoke crazy statements and acted more strangely than he previously had. When the Rabbi and I tried to talk him into selling everything in the barn to pay his bills, he put his clenched fist up to my cheek and told me to quit, or I would be tempting him to kill me and the rabbi as well. The rabbi was standing right next to me, and he motioned for me to quit. We both got out of his way and decided it was all a wasted effort on our part, but God had a plan.

Becca had not paid him any money during her stay, to my knowledge, nor did she do any work for him, so he had her locked out of the property by putting a chain and lock on the fence gate, keeping her RV and me locked inside the property. Fortunately for her, she was helped by the rabbi after she called the sheriff's department to investigate the lockout. When the sheriff came, they saw Bear in his polyester suit and combed hair and sweet, pleasant demeanor and decided "us women" were at fault for persecuting this sweet old man, and they left. The rabbi hooked up Becca's RV to her truck and told her to drive out while he kept Bear busy in an argument. Everyone else who had been staying there left earlier, leaving me behind. I learned months later that Becca died not long after she left there.

My car was broken down, unable to start, so I had it towed off into town to an auto repair shop, telling Bear I would be back when it was fixed, or he would not have let me go. The repair shop quoted me six hundred dollars just to get it started, which I knew I could not pay. Reluctantly, I called Rodney, my son-in-law, who came and started the car in minutes in the repair shop's lot and drove it off for further repair at the farm with me and the grandboys following behind. All my belongings were still at Bear's, and I knew I had to go back to retrieve them at some point.

The last few weeks I was living at Bear's property, he revealed he had PTSD, bipolar disease, prostate cancer, and a severe heart problem, among other things. He expressed he was tired and wanted to go back into the Mafia once again and be able to execute and murder people again as he did before. He said he enjoyed killing people and missed the action. Obviously, something had triggered in his mind, for he said the military taught him how to kill, and he enjoyed it. Supposedly, he only had a few months to live.

The rabbi had made secret arrangements for me to go to a safe house, not a government safe house but a moldy burned-out mobile home hidden away in the woods off the beaten path and difficult to find. Rabbi took me to meet the owners, who were in the process of painting over the fire and mold damages. Rabbi wasn't allowed to move me off the property by stern warning from Bear, or he would be killed.

Very reluctantly, I called my daughter, *again*, who thought I was a lost case to begin with, and asked for help to get me out of Bear's property. She made arrangements for all three of my older grandsons to meet me somewhere, and together, we made a surprise visit to Bear's property so he could not plan anything ahead of time. He truly was surprised to see me with the three *big* boys and became sweet and docile.

The boys loaded me up very quickly, and we drove off, with Bear watching, and then unloaded my stuff at my new safe house. I left explicit instructions with them not to tell anyone where I was. I changed my cell phone number and did not contact anyone, except Elizabeth's family and my doctors, for one year while hiding out in the woods. I had had enough!

All the while I was with Bear, I believed in my heart the Lord had sent me there for a purpose. I was very grateful the Lord was using me to help this man who was falling away from God's grace. At the end, when I cried out to God again, I heard the Lord's still, small voice saying that He was giving Bear another chance to turn away from evil and do good. If he refused my and the rabbi's help and did not comply with the plan God had given him, I was to leave and shake the dust off my feet. Last I heard, Rabbi was never able to change Bear's mind or heart and left him alone to his own devises.

Looking back, I had been led to a debilitating place, leaving me more dependent on Adonai (the Lord) than ever before. My eyes have been opened to my own behavior when I had found I had been deceived and used by friends I was bent on helping or assisting. When the truth became known to me, I was devastated and strongly desired wisdom, understanding, and discernment. So I sought the Lord to request these things of Him. What I viewed as a restoration place with Bear was not, but I was able to appreciate the surrounding beauty of the land. Adonai was ever so present at dawn, sunset,

146

and in-between with caressing winds and the peaceful silence of rural country living. Cut off from the mainstream, I spend my spare time reading His Word and drawing closer to Him with thanksgiving in my heart. Even though I have sinned by my thoughts and tongue, Adonai has not abandoned me but still leads me beside the still waters. He lifts me up on wings like eagles.

Yet when I fall and sin again, He is there to remind me of my folly and lead me back on the straight and narrow path to Him. He is preparing a place for me on earth right now but also a place in His kingdom where there shall be no sorrow, tears, fear, or sickness—only peace, joy, happiness, and a new body without pain and suffering.

While I was in the safe house in the woods, I was driving every other week to the farm to get my mail. On one occasion in the second year in the woods while I was driving, I felt I suddenly came out of a daydream and realized I had drool on my chin. When I mentioned it to Elizabeth and Rodney, they were alarmed, and they stated I could no longer drive my car, and they took my car keys, saying one of the boys would have to drive me back home and stay with me because it was too dangerous for me to drive or be alone. They thought I was having strokes or passing out at the wheel, which I did not believe. There was not enough conversation on the matter to satisfy me or make it okay with me. I was absolutely devastated. I didn't understand why they were so upset, and I felt they were being controlling and punishing me. In one moment, my freedom, my independence, my way of life were taken from me. I felt like less than a person, a failure, not good for anything or anyone—a burden! Why did God allow this to happen?

My job as caregiver I was working in that town was over, having to quit without proper notice. Then came the doctor appointments, per Elizabeth's insistence, to check my brain, resulting in a five-day stay in the hospital with wires stuck to my head. Along with that, the neurologist stated I should not drive until all tests were done, further debilitating me. Remembering how mold could affect a person's body and mind, I was convinced I had been affected by living in the moldy condition. I was so very angry with Elizabeth and Rodney and very upset for ever saying anything about daydreaming.

I became despondent and lonely in the woods, for the boys had schooling and jobs to attend and could not stay. They kept my car. However, I enjoyed my privacy there and tried to make the best of it. I just couldn't go anywhere. Walking was too dangerous with all the wildlife there in the woods, even in the light of day. But I did enjoy seeing all the deer families stroll on by about fifty feet from the house.

To keep my spirit up, I evangelized the Jewish woman who owned the residence I was in. I loaned her books on Judaism and taught her some of the Sabbath prayers. We celebrated the Jewish feasts together. To this day, she rejoices in her Judaism and shares what she has learned with all her adult relatives who have rejected her newfound position in the Lord. She continues to teach her grandchildren what she knows and is now practicing Messianic Judaism, which the grandchildren have embraced. We have kept in touch these last few years.

Sewing has been a special gift to me all my life from the Lord. I kept busy sewing quilts for birthday gifts for everyone in my family, loving and enjoying every moment of it. Yet I still missed my daily trips to the YMCA to work out and my wonderful trips to HEB to shop or just looking around on the town square. My independence, my adventures, my freedom were gone, stolen from me. Did I say freedom? What freedom did I have hiding from people and life in the woods?

After two years in the woods at my hiding place, the owners' well water pump broke, and I was again facing no water at all. After relaying this information to my daughter Elizabeth, the very next day, she came with all the children, and they packed me up and took me back to the farm. I hated that I had another move in this manner without prayer and planning or being involved in that decision to move again. Yet I was unable to drive or walk anywhere to get water or another place to live during this time.

Almost one year after my car was taken, when doctors could not find anything physically or mentally wrong with me according to their venue, I took it upon myself to get my car back and start driving again. I discovered my confidence in driving and general day-today living was shattered. Fear came back upon me, and I questioned everything I had to do. No work was I able to qualify for, and much pain and bodily dysfunction returned due to lack of exercise, not walking, being inactive, sitting a lot, and fear. I felt like I aged ten years within that year. Heaviness was upon me, pushing me downward like a spiral. I was slowly losing my physical capabilities.

I had to forgive myself for allowing myself to be subdued and deceived. Likewise, I had to forgive Elizabeth and Rodney for abruptly, harshly, I thought, disrupting my life in the manner they took it over. I felt I was being punished for just being me. Trust was broken. There was no intimacy for me with anyone to speak truth without severe consequences. Again, I felt like, *Why should I go on living like this? For whom? For what reason? When will I learn to stop listening and believing the lies of the devil?* That's exactly what had happened. The adversary took over because we left the door open for him to enter. The devil comes to destroy families by his lies. We did not know or understand that we had opened the door to the devil. But my perseverance for a better life and wanting to get closer to the Lord still took hold of me.

Now in 2019, I find intimacy and adventure by going to bed early and feeling the luxury of one hundred percent cotton sheets, pillows, and comforter, caressing and snuggling my body as I read a good, enlightening Christian book depicting events of our heroes of ancient times (David, Judah, Enoch, Jasher, etc.) and holding conversations with God, Yeshua (Jesus), and the Ruach haKodesh (the Holy Spirit), driving into the countryside during the daytime, looking at God's creation and visualizing my dreams that could still materialize.

Elizabeth had moved me back to the farm since Rodney was still away working in another state. One week later, she said I had to be gone by the end of the coming week because Rodney was returning home, and there was no room for me, so I called my friend Mandy in Florida, and said I was available for a visit. After she extended the invitation to come, I accepted and prepared to leave. I felt like and actually was a homeless person, an old lady now just floating around, bruised and weary. I bought myself a bus ticket to Florida and left. I will tell you more of this trip in the next chapter.

When I arrived back at the farm from Florida about two months later, Elizabeth said I could not stay with them anymore, for Rodney was returning home again from another out-of-state job. So that weekend, I attended a local church down the street from the farm. A woman in the congregation heard my plea for a place to stay. She made arrangements with a deaf woman one block from my farm who had a spare room to rent.

Upon viewing the property I did not like it, for it was very dark with only a minibath window in the bedroom, yet it was four walls and ceiling of shelter, which I was grateful for. She had a deaf pit bull dog, which was not housebroken or trained to follow commands, which I found scary. I continued my search for a better place without all the stress of having to use a flashlight to walk from room to room in her house due to all the windows being covered up dark, for she would only use the electric lighting in the house sparingly!

During one of my searches, I came upon a development for senior citizens and decided to check it out. The cost was way more than I thought I could afford. After praying over it overnight, I decided I really needed to settle for a while and felt this was where the Lord was placing me, according to Psalm 23. Even though the rent took more than half of my Social Security check, I felt I could trust the Lord for all my other needs.

Within two weeks, I moved into one of their very large one-bedroom fourplex built in what was once green pastures, beside the still waters of the lake and trails next door. I had peace at last. There was tranquility and quiet, a time for me to rest and seek the Lord that I may get back on my feet. I thanked God for where He was taking me. I am finally at peace, or so I thought for the first month.

After I moved to the senior complex, one of my neighbors came over to introduce herself to me and to find out what I was all about. After inviting her into my apartment and her looking around, she left and gave me her card, saying she was a pastor. One month later, this very same woman started harassing me and telling the neighbors I was making her sick with essential oils and candles and using the spices she saw on my counter to cook up a terrible odor, causing her to be sick. I never thought I had to explain to people why I have spices and herbs in my kitchen. Surely there are other folks who love to cook and create new recipes like I do. As far as having candles in my home, which millions of people have also, I use them mostly for display in my menorahs and candle holders, for I like that decor.

This harassment went on for several months. During that time, she kept calling the police, asking them to come to investigate inside my home to see what was causing the awful smell she thought I was sending into her attached apartment. The officers could never find anything wrong in my apartment and said they were sorry for the trouble. She sent me harassing texts, saying I was into witchcraft and was a demon, and she was telling the neighbors not to speak to me because I was a demon in her opinion. The complex personnel copied her texts she sent to me onto their phones as a record. She continued to harass me for months. No longer did I feel safe or very peaceful.

> Now My soul has become troubled; and what shall I say, "Father, save Me from this hour"? But for this purpose I came to this hour. (John 12:27 NASB, Jesus's call to obedience)

One day, this woman followed me in her car as I was leaving the complex to go shopping. There was a police car at a stop, talking to a person, and I turned in behind him, but he didn't notice me and drove off. Meanwhile, she saw I was trying to get the officer's attention, and she left. When I came back home, I decided to get her license plate number and make of her car in case this happened again. She saw me standing by her car, writing down her license plate number, and came at me, yelling from the neighbors down the block. She hit my arm and pushed me down, causing me to fall on all fours and knocking the pen and paper out of my hand. She made a cut on my arm that bled when she hit me. Police were called by management, but officers were not cooperative with me or the complex managers as they believed the woman's story that I was harassing her over mine and the complex managers.

After much to do and my appearing in court, this woman was finally evicted. She had made it clear in court that she did not like me for my religion and beliefs: Judaism. Again, I failed the Lord by letting fear overtake me during those harassing months. Surely I have finally learned the lesson of trusting in God and not in myself. I pray for her eyes to be opened to the truth of the Word, for forgiveness, and for her salvation.

Since she left, the complex has been very peaceful and quiet, and those tenants around our fourplex have been much happier and quieted in their spirit, enjoying each other's company and mine. Now it's another time for me to ask forgiveness from the Lord for not trusting in Him and to rest in His Word and in His arms.

Bad things happen to good people and bad people alike, for we are living in a fallen world. Yet God is able and willing to turn the bad, the evil, that happens to us around for good.

> I remember my affliction and my wandering, the bitterness and the gall. I remember them, and my soul is downcast within me. Yet this I call to mind and therefore I have hope: Because of the Lord's great love we are not consumed, for his compassions never fail. They are new every morning; great is your faithfulness. I say to myself, "The Lord is my portion; therefore I will wait for him." The Lord is good to those whose hope is in him, to the one who seeks him; it is good to wait quietly for the salvation of the Lord. (Lamentations 3:19–26 NASB, Afflictions)

> But realize this, that in the last days difficult times will come. For men will be lovers of self, lovers of money, boastful, arrogant, revilers, disobedient to parents, ungrateful, unholy, unloving, irreconcilable, malicious gossips, without self-control, brutal, haters of good, treacherous, reckless, conceited, lovers of pleasure rather than

lovers of God, holding to a form of godliness, although they have denied its power. Avoid such men as these. (2 Timothy 3:1–5 NASB, Difficult Times)

This event in my life describes many in our society today. We should not give in to society's pressure to conform. There are many people even in the church and at work or home who appear to have godliness in appearance, who know the Christian Word or doctrine, which makes them appear good, but their true attitudes of love, faith, and worship are lacking. Their daily, weekly behavior gives them away. Be alert! For God will reveal them all in His time.

> The eyes of the LORD are toward the righteous
> And His ears are open to their cry.
> The face of the LORD is against evildoers,
> To cut off the memory of them from the earth.
> The righteous cry, and the LORD hears
> And delivers them out of all their troubles.
> The LORD is near to the brokenhearted
> And saves those who are crushed in spirit.
> Many are the afflictions of the righteous,
> But the LORD delivers him out of them all. (Psalm
>   34:15–19 NASB, God's promise of peace)

CHAPTER 16

Florida Nightmare

Now comes the saga of my Florida trip, one which may cause you to fall off your chair from laughter, at least the bus trip portion of this story. When I left for Florida in July 2017, I took a bus due to lack of funds to pay for a last-minute airline ticket. Happy that Mandy had invited me to come, I looked forward to the trip. One of my grandsons dropped me off and carried my luggage onto the bus.

I got a seat next to a young black boy, who became dismayed when I sat down next to him. He turned his body to face the window and started rapping, saying, "I poor. I poor. I need a job. I need a job. I poor. I poor. I need a job." He would not look at me even when I introduced myself and asked his name. He just kept looking out the window, rapping, "I poor. I poor. I need a job." He never spoke a word to me or looked at me the entire time we were seated together.

When the bus came to the first stop, he got up and jumped over me to get out as fast as he could! I prayed a prayer for him to have peace and find work loudly enough that he could hear while the bus was traveling. I pray he's been able to deal with his situation in life. Not wanting to insult or upset him, I did not pray for his salvation in his hearing.

We changed buses there, and I got a seat next to the window this time. A young woman came and sat next to me, who introduced herself as Rebeccah, saying she was just released from prison. She was on her way to a halfway house before going out into the world. She was quite talkative and happy to be out of prison to start a new life. She said she found Jesus while in prison and accepted Him as her Lord and Savior. She wanted to make a new life and was hoping to see her young children after such a long time.

All the while she was talking, I was making sure to clutch my bag, thinking I was about to get taken by a slight of hand, then I realized what I was doing and relaxed. I was uncomfortable but didn't want to make her uncomfortable. She continued with her life story until it was time for her to get off at her stop. We prayed together for her future and restoration of her family and life. I asked the Lord to pour blessings on her and keep her on the straight and narrow path. She arrived at her destination and got off the bus, strange encounters to say the least. She is still on my prayer list for daily prayer.

The next person who sat next to me was a middle-aged man whose name escapes me. He kept rubbing and scratching his body parts, saying he just came from a rented apartment that had bedbugs he couldn't get rid of. He took out photos of himself, almost completely in the nude, to show me his bites and expressed how angry he was about it. He said he was going to meet a friend who told him he was studying to be a terrorist and wanted him to join him to be a partner (in crime?). Really? Where did this guy come from?

He kept scratching himself so much I began to think I was getting his bugs on me. His conversation was of complete hatred of America, people in general, and general frustration in life. He wanted to get even with people who troubled him.

When the bus stopped for rest, I reported him to the bus driver so he could report him to authorities and have him checked out at the next stop (as a possible terrorist). He refused to let me pray for him. He stated religion was of no value to anyone. I wondered that myself from time to time. Certainly, he was a very troubled person. By this time, I was feeling itchy and imagining bugs clawing onto me as we sat in our seats. I tried telling myself it's just my imagination, but it wasn't working.

The trip was both humorous and disgusting. When I arrived at my destination in Florida, Mandy was there waiting for me, along with her two grandchildren. Feeling contaminated with bedbugs from the guy on the bus, I refused to get in her car without changing clothes, which I did quickly. Mandy, I discovered, had changed into a different person due to chronic severe stress and chaos in her house. She just wanted to sleep all the time when she was not catering to her spoiled granddaughter, who didn't want to be there with her. She fought with Mandy constantly, trying to get her way, and usually won by wearing her down. She had been rescued from the streets, yet her granddaughter had a face of a naive, sweet all-American girl next door. Such deception!

Mandy's husband of over two years gave her problems even before they married, but Mandy refused to see it. He used her compassionate, loving heart until she was almost dead in spirit herself. He died of cancer after a three-year battle, all the while being taken care of by Mandy until his final admittance into a hospital. I could see she was completely worn out mentally, physically, and spiritually.

While I was there visiting her, manifestations of demons appeared twice on my bed to torture and fight one of her beloved cats who had made my bed her resting place. In horror, I saw the cat's eyes enlarge, mouth open, and claws come out fighting the invisible demon. Mandy could not believe it when I told her of it. She thought I was making it up for some reason, to my own despair. There was so much demon activity or evil atmosphere inside the house, I tried to spend much of my time outdoors.

Mandy flatly rejected my help, except for washing the dishes and feeding the animals. I tried to talk her out of staying there, to move back to Texas, but she couldn't bring herself to even think of the idea. She just wanted to stay in bed and sleep. I prayed in the spirit quietly every day I was there that the Lord would open her eyes to see the truth of her situation, to give her strength to overcome and take charge of her life. She was embittered about her husband dying on her and not leaving her anything, not even the house they were living in. She said she was still in love with him but angry at him. She was not able to forgive him.

I grieved for her, for she was not the person I had known through the previous years. She seemed spent and exhausted. These scriptures brought me comfort, but I was unable to share them with her.

> My heavenly Father will also do the same to you, if each of you does not forgive his brother from your heart. (Matthew 18:35 NASB)

> Be kind to one another, tender-hearted, forgiving each other, just as God in Christ also has forgiven you. (Ephesians 4:32 NASB)

> Yet those who wait for the LORD
> Will gain new strength;
> They will mount up with wings like eagles,
> They will run and not get tired,
> They will walk and not become weary. (Isaiah 40:31 NASB)

Mandy was suffering greatly with pain, depression, oppression, insomnia, exhaustion and was just plain miserable. Her husband died in November of 2015. She had put up Christmas decorations and a huge fake tree before he died. It was all still up when I arrive in July 2017. I told her I would help her take it down, but she refused. The house seemed very dark; blinds on the windows never were opened. I could feel spirits roaming around. She wanted to keep the memory of those last few weeks with her husband when he was alive.

She was in deep oppression. I couldn't help her. I did not know what further to do. She didn't want rescuing. She was struggling with her seventeen-year-old granddaughter, whom she had taken in, hoping to give her direction in her life. The granddaughter needed more help, professional help, than Mandy was able to give her. The granddaughter tried manipulating me to get me to oppose Mandy so she could get her way. Eventually, Mandy finally found another relative in another state, who said they would come and pick her up and take her to their horse ranch used to rehabilitate individuals. This happened a couple months after I left Florida for home. That left Mandy alone in her haunted house, which she refused to acknowledge.

Two months into my visit there, a severe storm was headed for the area Mandy was living. Elizabeth called me, saying I needed to get out of Florida immediately. The TV news made it look extremely bad for the area we were in, so I charged an air flight and headed back to DFW. I felt the weight of the oppression and didn't feel like I could handle another bus ride back to DFW by this time. Mandy was not concerned about the impending weather, only enduring for one more day in her dead husband's house, which she still had due to Florida laws concerning marital property at a spouse's death.

About four months after I returned home, Mandy was murdered, beaten. She was dragged into the garage and shot dead three times. Her granddaughter's boyfriend, who lived down the street from Mandy, was arrested and charged, according to the local news. Had it not been for the approaching storm, I would have chosen to stay longer to try and help her and may have found myself somewhere in this scenario. I can't even imagine her or my life ending this way.

Mandy was my closest friend, and I had missed her greatly when she moved to Florida. We would call each other and talk for hours, but I never went to her funeral, nor have I been able to cry over her sudden brutal death or loss of her friendship. I could not save her. Perhaps it was her total rejection of my help that I was never able to shed tears over her death. Only God knows. Perhaps it was not meant for me to rescue her. Since she was Christian and loved the Lord, I can only hope she is home with Christ—no more pain and suffering. I still think about her a lot and continue praying for her salvation, grateful that I was called back to DFW.

> For if you forgive others for their transgressions, your heavenly Father will forgive you. But if you do not forgive others, then your Father will not forgive your transgressions. (Matthew 6:14–15 NASB, Forgiveness)

From beginning to end, we face tests, trials, and all sorts of hills and mountains and valleys of adventures. We may face dissatisfaction, hardships, temptations, even violence. My successes or failures are determined by how I deal with them through my actions to these circumstances. Each one of us has been given our own promised land (goals, ideals, success, etc.), and it is up to us to seek God, Jesus, and the Holy Spirit on how to get there and avoid the pitfalls of the evil one, which many of us fall into.

Through my life, I have fallen prey many times, not understanding why it could happen to me. It seemed I was not learning from my mistakes but rather repeating them. This trip showed me how we can go through life blind or in denial. Observing Mandy in her home was like I was looking at myself in the past—a reflection of myself, a real eye-opener. Truly, we have been given the power to overcome the evil powers that come against us. We need to learn how to use what God has given us: His Word in our daily life.

In the next chapter, my daughter takes center stage in my life, for I had left Florida and gone back to Texas to try and settle somewhere on my own.

CHAPTER 17

My Daughter, My Enemy?

Elizabeth, my daughter, was conceived in Giessen, Germany, while I and Forrest, my first husband, were stationed there in the army. It was a wonderful place to be, and Forrest and I were happy learning the ways of that land. Just a couple of months before our return to America, we discovered we were pregnant. We were both very happy! I could hardly wait to wear a maternity dress to show everyone I was pregnant and really, really going to have a baby. I walked purposefully pushing my stomach outward so everyone could see I was pregnant. How exciting that was for me.

Upon our arrival to our home in San Juan, California, we found our renters had left the house in complete disarray and filthy. Fortunately, our friends helped us get it cleaned up, and we began to get ready for our baby's birth. We discovered the baby was going to be a girl but had not picked a name for her yet. I started making clothes for her since I sewed a lot and was having fun preparing for this much wanted child.

We decided the house wasn't big enough being only seven hundred square feet. We purchased a three-bedroom, two-bath home—a fixer-upper—in a better neighborhood. I was working for an electronics company in the insurance department, processing employee medical claims with another woman, Liz, who took special interest in helping me improving my work skills and personal life habits. She was almost past the age of childbearing and always wanted a daughter but never had any children. Liz took it upon herself to gift us with a complete baby layette: crib, linens, clothes, toys, etc. I was overwhelmed. Forrest felt like he missed out on shopping and making selections for the baby. He had gone back to work at TWA as a baggage handler and back to drinking, coming home drunk a lot.

When it was time for the birth, it was Liz who bought the wonderful gifts for us, who took me to the hospital, and who was there for me during the birth. The whereabouts of Forrest was unknown at the time. The two of us joked about calling the baby Elizabeth. When it came time, I did name her Elizabeth after my faithful friend Lizzy.

Elizabeth was born three weeks early and breech. They put me out (under anesthesia), so I never saw the birth in process. Hours later, they brought this tiny, little bundle to me. She was so cute and precious. I was afraid to hold her for fear of hurting her. I wanted to nurse her, but after trying for two days in the hospital and her losing a whole pound down to 5.3 pounds in weight, I gave up. The nurses didn't know why I wasn't able to nurse and didn't know how to instruct me. I cried out of disappointment that I could not do that for her or even for myself. So she became a bottle baby. She became allergic to regular milk and various other foods, which complicated things for us. I felt I was to blame for that outcome.

I became depressed and retreated into postpartum depression for eleven months. My doctor never diagnosed me as having this problem perhaps because they had not studied this illness at that time. I was afraid to hold her and kept thinking she was going to die because I was not a good mother, for I had gone back to work as a postal carrier within six weeks of her birth. Forrest was not making enough to cover all expenses and his bar bills too. We desperately needed the money to pay the bills. I was physically and mentally ill with no one to turn to. I broke down on the job and was forced to quit or get fired. While I was working, we had a sitter for Elizabeth.

However, Forrest spent a lot of time with her when he was home. He loved her very much, and she looked just like him.

Within the first six months, her pediatrician found problems with her legs and hips. They had not developed fully, and he said she would have to wear a body brace for a few months to keep her movement still while her bones continued to grow. When that didn't work, she was sent to an orthopedic specialist at Stanford Hospital. They did surgery on her right hip, placing a steel bar in the area that needed to stay still, and then put her in a full-body cast from her armpits to her toes for eight weeks. This was to insure she would be able to walk.

Eventually, Elizabeth did walk but with a limp, for the bones did not grow or form as the doctor predicted. My grandmother's Italian doctor told me our family had a generational hip disease (a curse) from Northern Italy. Years later, we learned it truly was a generational curse. I was born with the same problem, as was my mother and grandfather, but not as severe.

While Elizabeth was in the hospital getting surgery and recovering, I had to work full-time. I had taken a job as a computer entry clerk, and I was the only person trained to do the job at a local bakery. It was imperative I be there every day to key in the daily orders from the vendors in the field as they called in, therefore tying me up so I could not be with her during the daytime working hours. We needed the money, or I would have had to go on the welfare rolls. I was only able to be with Elizabeth early in the morning and after work.

The nursing staff did not take kindly to my not being there with Elizabeth during the day and nights and let me know in so many words and disgusting looks. Before Elizabeth had the surgery, I had separated from Forrest and took an apartment on my own with her. I had to work since he was not paying child support or alimony. Forrest had gone to see her a few times in the hospital, which helped.

Elizabeth suffered much pain and aloneness and seemed to have withdrawn from me. When I took her home, there was no way for me to alleviate the pain inside the cast. I could see her anger at me for not helping her. I had to keep her on the floor on top of a blanket all the time or in her crib. She would cry and scream for help, "Mommy,

Mommy," when she was only a year and a half old. She developed a temper, needless to say. I didn't know what to do for her, and there were no manuals on what to do. It was difficult holding her, so I had to lay or sit on the floor with her. She would get mad and throw her toys at me. From this time forward, there was a tangible separation between us.

We were both so relieved when the cast came off. Then came rehab and therapy to get her to walk. The doctors even tried electrical shoes that would give her a little shock if she didn't put her heel down first when walking. She hated to walk, and I hated to see her suffer, so that was abruptly discontinued. For the rest of the next eight years, she saw doctors regularly as well as her father on appointed times, for we were now divorced. Forrest did not believe there was anything wrong with Elizabeth to begin with physically or mentally.

The years went on, and I had remarried a few years after my divorce from Forrest. He also remarried not long after the divorce to a slightly older woman.

Elizabeth and I had found a Baptist church to attend, where I met my second husband, Drake, and was living with him before our marriage. Forrest and his new wife reported me to California Child Protective Services that Elizabeth was not being taken care of properly. However, pastors reported to CPS that Elizabeth was well adjusted and in a good, loving Christian home, for Forrest and his new wife had requested an investigation from CPS to gain custody of Elizabeth, stating she was in a bad home environment.

The school officials and teachers reported to CPS, "She was an excellent student, a capable thinker, bright, but manipulative and had some behavior problems. She was more mature and sophisticated than other 8 year olds, and very aware she is a female."

The pastors reported that "Elizabeth was a sensuous child in her own right. Elizabeth used the two-parent situation to manipulate her needs and whims trying to appear innocent. Her mother still carried her in her arms when she was in kindergarten and first grade."

Remembering when I was under five years old and older, there was a lack of touching, embracing; no kind, loving words to edify me were ever spoken. My parents reinforced my worthlessness: "born a mistake," "a girl instead of a boy," "a troublemaker" all echoed in my head. I did not want this for Elizabeth. When we were together, I would hold her on my lap, kiss her cheeks, and call her words of endearing love—in some ways an overbearing parent yet very lacking at the same time. I had no idea how to be a parent.

Even when Elizabeth was twelve, I remember having her on my lap, hugging her, which infuriated Drake. He would tell her to get off my lap and said, "You're too old for that!" He was jealous of my affections toward her.

I was a shame-based parent, and despite the hugs and kisses I gave Elizabeth, she still suffered abuse by reason of my own shame. My shame became hers. My own need for love and hugs were huge. Elizabeth became my possession and my idol, for I desperately needed her and wanted her in my life. She was my only reason to go on living. There was no God in my life at that time.

All these reports from various sources came about when Forrest and I were fighting over custody of Elizabeth in 1981. The reports were submitted to the court for judgment. I won the first battle in court.

Looking back now in 2019, we all believed the lies that were handed down from the various reporters—i.e., pastors, teachers, counselors, investigators, etc. I believe it would be accurate to say none of these professional people were trained in or had any awareness of the spiritual person nor of hidden abuse or dysfunctional families—yes, even pastors. They could not see or feel Elizabeth's heart, her soul, or mine for that matter. If they could, they may have given a much different report. They were blinded to the emptiness and longing in her soul...to the extreme love she possessed for people, to the underdog, and to nature.

Her acting out at school and church was misinterpreted, and she received no help. From time to time, her school officials would call me to come and view Elizabeth's behavior in class without her knowing I was observing. She would always be sitting at her desk, quietly watching the students around her, not causing any problems, which angered me that they would accuse her of making trouble. I was blinded and couldn't see it. Elizabeth had been deeply hurt.

She felt abandoned, confused, rejected, abused, and she inherited the trauma I had been living with. So many times, she acted out through her distorted vision. Other times, she was well-behaved and seemed to be the perfect child to me.

So I decided to find a Christian school to transfer her to. I found one about twenty minutes away from home and enrolled her in it and drove her to and from school every day. Mind you, I was not saved, nor did I understand spiritual matters but *thought* it might be better for her. Within a couple of weeks, Elizabeth told me she was saved and was praying for me to get saved. I didn't comprehend what she was talking about. I thought I was a wonderful parent at the time only because I tried so hard to do what I thought was right. Unfortunately, even when I saw the error of my ways, I was hopeless and helpless to change anything on my own. I had no true spiritual knowledge yet, only Bible stories for kids. Life itself was a disaster for us, and I hated it.

Not long after I gave Elizabeth to her dad, I found salvation miraculously, as per my story of being led to Hawaii in a previous chapter. You see, it is a lie from hell when someone tells you God can't use you or talk to you unless you are saved or born again. God used and caused donkeys to talk for His purposes, as mentioned in the Bible. It was God who directed me to put Elizabeth in that Christian school that led us both to the Lord in His own timing and in His own way. God truly works in mysterious ways.

The years Elizabeth was with me, we struggled to survive and be healthy happy human beings. At age twelve, Elizabeth had gone to live with her dad and her stepmother, Janet, for I gave her up for her own protection from Drake. At age fifteen, her dad passed away with malignant melanoma. She recounted to me of staying home from school many times to take care of her dying father in Janet's place, for Janet was also sick much of the time and in the hospital.

Right after her father died, she and Janet got an attorney and tried to take me to court, stipulating Elizabeth wanted to divorce me as her mother. Her stepmother, Janet, wanted to ensure that she receive the Social Security death benefits for Elizabeth from Forrest's death and not Elizabeth's birth mother. I never went to court or acknowledged the legal paperwork I received because I simply could not handle that and Drake too. So I did nothing about it, ignoring the whole situation. This resulted in Elizabeth's staying with Janet for the rest of her teen years.

Elizabeth's disgust and resentment of me only intensified through those years. There were some visitations with her on my part during that time while I was still living with Drake, who had abused us both. When she turned eighteen and graduated from high school, I volunteered to send her to Oral Roberts University in Tulsa, Oklahoma, to medical school if she desired to go, for she had a dream of being a doctor or nurse practitioner. I agreed to pay the first semester if she would find scholarships for herself. She accepted, so Drake and I took her to the airport to see her off.

At ORU in Tulsa, the Lord placed Elizabeth in the same dormitory, in the same room I had stayed the year before while I attended a pastor's conference. I had prayed over that very room and visualized Elizabeth attending and being there in that room. That could only have been an act of God to place her in the very room I stayed. Every month, I would send her a care package of sorts with clothes and gifts. It ended after a few months from pressure from Drake. Not long after that, I left Drake again.

In September 1988, I flew to Bent Oak, Oklahoma, and purchased property with two homes on it. I gave Elizabeth permission to live in one, but she was in her early wanderings, trying to survive herself. ORU closed their medical school, and she left. I tried to befriend her but to no avail. She was still angry and bitter toward me for her traumatic upbringing and my leaving her and her dad. I thought she had every right to be angry for what she went through.

When I packed up in December of 1988 and drove to Bent Oak, I moved into one of the homes. The trip driving there and situation with Elizabeth not wanting to stay in one of my homes, I became even more mentally out of whack and started taking more prescription drugs to cope. That turned me into an even more unstable person, a whacko! We were two abused, misguided, dysfunctional people struggling as best we knew how to survive, to find peace. Where was God? Did we ever call on Him? No!

Elizabeth found her way to a tiny church group pastored by a woman and had befriended a young girl there who was questioning her existence as a female. Elizabeth was all too quick to minister to her and stay with her. The woman pastor Batty proved to be a fraud as time went on.

Every opportunity that came Elizabeth's way to hurt me or come against me, she did, not knowing the devil or evil forces were propelling her that way to cause her and myself harm. I remind you, the devil, Satan, is the accuser of God's people. He is the prince and ruler of evil spirits. "The devil comes to steal, kill and destroy. I [Jesus] came that they may have life and have it abundantly" (John 10:10 NIV). Satan is an expert at deception and breaking up families. Our eyes and minds were on our troubles, not so much on the Lord.

> Then they cried out to the Lord in their trouble,
> and he brought them out of their distress.
> He stilled the storm to a whisper;
> the waves of the sea[a] were hushed. (Psalm
> 107:28–29 NASB; Turmoil, Confusion)

There were a few times we actually found help with each other by staying together, going to church together, and cleaning house together. One day, we found many stored glass jars, dishes, and cups, and we took them to the middle of the street and threw them hard against the curb to relieve our tension. It worked only for that moment. We soon parted ways again.

Elizabeth enrolled in a medical tech school in Bent Oak but within a few months needed to move because of a volatile divorce from her first husband. She transferred to another campus of the same school in Arlington, Texas. We both drove down together to Arlington and rented an apartment. Our relationship as friends was only viable when there was a need.

This is when Elizabeth met Rodney through a telephone dating service. They hit it off right away and eventually were married. I had moved out and gone back to Bent Oak to resolve my property issues. We continued to disagree on many issues and argue. She had always been a very strong-willed, determined person from tod-dlerhood. Rather than argue or debate, I would walk away irritated, hurt, and angry that I could not hold my own or be more forceful. I usually would feel condemnation and shame and strive to get away by myself, away from her and people. I refused to hold a conversa-tion with her or anyone else who brought me down. She hated that response from me. She wanted me to be stronger...*like her.*

So through the years, Elizabeth and Rodney had many chil-dren—ten, in fact—and she had no desire to stop bearing. At times, we tried to come together but would always end up in disappoint-ment. Mean words were spoken to one another or complete silence.

Somehow, whatever I spoke to Elizabeth would be understood totally different than what I meant. It was as if we spoke two differ-ent languages and did not understand one another. Many times, she would deny a statement she made the day before and accuse me of lying or making it up, saying, "I never said that!"

I would just give up and think, *Who is this person?*

Without explanation, one time in front of all the children, she came at me in the kitchen, yelling at me to admit that I was a liar. She kept it up, and she and the children were all waiting for me to answer. I gave in and yelled back, "Yes, I am a liar!" just to shut her up. I couldn't say, "No, I'm not!" I ingested the pain of her words, and humiliation and anger set in. She got what she wanted with no explanation to me, and I didn't ask the reason for her questioning accusation, but the fact that the children witnessed the questioning was humiliating for me and caused more separation.

Elizabeth has always had a loud voice, harsh and belittling for me, especially when speaking to me in front of the children. It always reminds me of my grandmother always yelling and cursing at me, belittling me. You can imagine how delighted the adversary was at those times, putting a wedge between us. Neither of us or the family had any idea why this was happening. Satan was taking us down *his* road to destroy us.

The curse, the wedge, was always between me, Elizabeth, Rodney, and the children. We did not know we were all being used by the adversary. The devil's goal is to break up families, to kill and destroy. He was doing a good job with us all the way back to my mother, father, and even grandparents' time. From the beginning, we were a very dysfunctional family, falling into the schemes of the devil. Why? How does this happen?

Lack of knowledge! The truth has been distorted through the generations, and lies have been passed down from generation to generation that we believe and live by, for no one told us otherwise. We will *fight* for those lies, for that is all we know. The wondrous times Elizabeth and I could have had in our early years are gone forever.

During the twelve years I had Elizabeth, I always worked, for we needed the income. Drake, my last husband, was not willing to support Elizabeth and me as needed, so I stepped up to the plate to pay for Elizabeth's Christian schooling, clothes, food, and my own needs. Some evenings, I would go to our church Bible classes with Drake. Elizabeth would come with us and stay in the kids' room, or at times, Elizabeth would choose to stay at home alone.

In my wounded mind, I felt I could trust her to be alone at home. That proved to be false thinking later on, for she would recount how afraid she was. As an adult, Elizabeth would question me as to why I left her alone. "Where were you?" She would recount stories to her children of things that happened in the past that I had no recollection of, stories I could not believe. But I stayed quiet so I would not be verbally refuted, especially in front of the children. Several times as an adult, she would tell me in anger that I was not her mother, that I was never a mother. That further enlarged the gap and wedge between us—Satan at work, of course, laughing to himself all the way.

When Elizabeth was born, neither the doctor nor the hospital gave me a manual on how to raise a child. What I never knew was that there really is a manual on how to raise children: *the Holy Bible!* No one in my family had ever read or used the Bible. It was a foreign dusty object mostly sitting on a shelf, if you could find it. The only time God was ever mentioned was as a curse word or scare tactic to control us.

So I admit I was not a good loving mother that I should have been, and now wish I could have been. For me, now at seventy-seven, there is still a gap (that I am working on closing) between me and my only daughter. Only God can heal the wounds, and He is because of who He is and, of course, our desire to close the gap. We only need to be open to receive what He has for us.

Forgiveness is a very big part of healing. We cannot go back and redo what has already taken place. We can only go forward. That's a choice we have to make. We can stay in the past and dwell on all the trauma and stagnate in bitterness and hate or just give up and stay in our hurts and unforgiveness and suffer, or we can choose to begin again where life finds us with a changed soft heart looking for newness in every new day that comes.

We will always have the memories that invade our space, which the adversary is expert at doing, but we have power and authority from God (*if you have given over your life to Him*) to push those memories aside. I had been under teachings that say if you still remember past hurts, you have never forgiven. That's false teaching. God is able to set His people free from their problems. Jesus calls those who are burdened to come to Him for relief and to show us the way of forgiveness. Elizabeth is *not* my enemy! The devil is.

> Come to Me, all who are weary and heavy-laden, and I will give you rest. Take My yoke upon you and learn from Me, for I am gentle and humble in heart, and YOU WILL FIND REST FOR YOUR SOULS. For My yoke is easy and My burden is light. (Matthew 11:28–30 NASB)

God is able to intervene and release us from various bondages and hurtful memories that weigh us down. Through faith in Jesus, our shackles can fall away. We can remember hurtful times without the hurt being imposed on us again. That's freedom! I would not be able to write this book if I had to take on the pain and suffering from the past. I can look at those times and be so thankful for where I am today: in the loving arms of Christ. There is hope and a way in Christ!

Sometimes it is hard to have hope because we are so despondent. To believe to hope again after having been let down by hoping in the past, we decide not to be hurt ever again. We make a decision to avoid ever being hurt again by refusing to hope ever again. If you are someone who expects the worst possible outcome of any situation, you are probably a pessimist who is afraid to believe for anything better. The real enemy here is the devil, our adversary who may be refusing to let go of you to keep you from hoping again.

There is so much more for Elizabeth and me to do in Christ. We have both been gifted with many talents that were meant to be used for the Lord for His glory. Thank God the blinders have been removed, and we can now see the light, the truth, and are now being renewed in spirit by His lovingkindness, grace, and mercy. We are *in the process* of receiving complete freedom from the past, from the enemy, through Jesus (Yeshua our Messiah) our healer. You cannot apply truth in your life unless you learn of it and understand what truth is. We are in the right place in God's perfect timing to be healed and to glorify God through His Word in our lives. Praise the Lord!

My mother, my father, all the way back to my grandparents and beyond were trapped in the lies of the devil, who distorts and brings illusions, which altered the God-given path of life they were meant to have. They were all in bondage, including myself. Many of us today are in bondage of one sort or another until we learn the truth and discover the way out.

When we are wronged by someone, we are not allowed to take revenge, return evil with evil, for God says "Never take your own revenge, beloved, but leave room for the wrath of God, for it is written, 'VENGANCE IS MINE, I WILL REPAY, says the Lord'" (Romans 12:19 NASB). I don't know of anything more powerful than giving your enemy over to Him to do as He pleases. *Wow!* We are instructed to overcome evil with good. When we take matters into our own hands, it is because we don't trust God to resolve the problem or situation on our behalf. It is lack of faith.

> For we wrestle not against flesh and blood, but against principalities, against powers, against the rulers of the darkness of this world, against spiritual wickedness in high places. (Ephesians 6:12 KJV)

So we should not be fighting with people: family, friends, neighbors, coworkers, or congregants—anyone. Have faith that God will carry the matter and resolve the problem in His time for our sake and His. Trust in Him!

> For there is nothing hidden that will not be disclosed, and nothing concealed that will not be known or brought out into the open. (Luke 8:17 KJV)

Don't be limited by the way you were raised. Speak to your future with positive, strong, bold words. Be positive, strong, and bold in your prayers to God regarding your future and what you would like to be and do. Don't be ashamed to ask for blessings like, "Bless me, Father, to overflowing so I can be a better blessing to others." Continue to speak blessings over yourself, being positive and bold no matter how you see yourself right now. God, who created you, sees you with His eyes as a wonderful creation and wants to bless you. Trust in Him!

CHAPTER 18

The Awakening

My entire life, to sum it all up, was one of searching for something...something, someone to fill the void, the emptiness. There was no purpose for my existence, I thought, especially after I lost my daughter. I hated life. I would ask myself, "Is there really a God who cares or loves me? Where is He?" I spent much time trying out various congregations, different denominations and secular organizations that would supposedly put me in touch with this higher power, but I couldn't find Him in any of them. "Where does God hang out? I need You, God!" I would cry out, but I couldn't hear a response most of the time, or at least that's what I thought.

Surely there's got to be more than this. I had answered so many altar calls and prayed the prayer of salvation so many times, but nothing seemed to change, except when I first received the Lord in Hawaii. *What else is there? What do I do now?* were constant questions in my mind, which various pastors and counselors were not answering. I would hear the same thing over and over again. It was more beneficial and enjoyable to me when I was taking Bible classes, learning His Word, but there was still a void in my being. I felt like I had heaviness on my shoulders all the time and was feeling incomplete. I believed and knew something was wrong with me, but what?

I didn't know. Why are some of the people in congregations enjoying singing and dancing to the Lord and enjoying life? They are just pretending they are happy was my conclusion. I can pretend and act just as happy, then I can look like one of them. Yet I knew in my heart they (many of them) were very sad, miserable people sitting in pews, chairs, or standing, waiting for the service to end so they could leave and go on to their miserably happy life.

After trying to minister and console a few of these people, I discovered I didn't have what they needed or answers to help them either. It made me feel inadequate, useless, a reject, just as I had been told by my parents and leaders through the years. I believed the lies of the devil all my life, which kept me going in pursuit of something else better. What, I had no idea.

Pastors and leaders in various denominations would often expose their own unhappiness or marital problems to the congregation over and over with the thought they were helping someone out without any scriptural resolve, but I seriously doubt it brought anyone closer to God or helped them in their situations. I didn't want to hear anymore, so I decided to get very involved in serving within the congregations, doing things I really enjoyed, like crafty arts within the children's church, teaching (what little I understood) of the Word, collecting and posting tithes, accounting, vacuuming floors, cleaning the restrooms, serving food, quilt making for fundraising, etc. The more I threw myself into the *works*, the less I felt the pain within me. I could smile and be happy just like everyone else, or so it appeared. This way, I didn't have time to sit in the pews and listen to others discontent or seemingly to me misguided teachings.

It seemed I always ended up having problems with the pastors and/or leaders, causing me to leave the church to save face or out of my disgust. Their wives always seemed to be irritated with me for just being in the congregation and for their husbands' talking with me. I never looked to have any *personal* relationships with those pastors or leaders other than as a working congregant, but the wives thought differently and even some of the pastors for just being myself. I had figured out that my looks were above average, but I never thought I was an extremely attractive woman who would cause these issues. I decided people (men particularly) of the church were not so godly after all and were just like any other guy at work or in the world. I believed *they* needed to repent, not me! I had lost all trust in them.

There were several years during my wanderings I simply did not attend church or seek the Lord out. What was the point? Brokenness and wounds prevailed. Selfishly, I wanted to nurture myself and do everything for myself. No one else, just me, me, *me!* That's all I cared about until I would recover to some degree and started the never-ending cycle of wondering and wanderings all over again. Saved, born again, filled with the Holy Spirit—I still struggled. There was an unwanted heaviness on my shoulders weighing me down besides an unquenchable drive to find, search for the solution.

Finally, in October 2016, during my latter wanderings and before my trip to Florida, I was drawn to a different Messianic Jewish congregation through my grandson, who was following the Lord very closely. It was a very small group of about twenty people. The leader of the group was from Venezuela. He spoke several languages and knew Hebrew. His teachings were so deep in the Word of God, especially with the book of Leviticus. It threw me deeper into the Word and understanding of it, and it developed a thirst for more.

After four years of Bible classes in two different congregations, I felt like I had wasted my time, missing out on the true meaning of the Word. This new congregation is what I had been looking for… real in-depth truth. Each week, the word got out about this leader called Joey Benami at Sukkat Shalom Messianic Congregation in Arlington, Texas. By December 2018, the congregation grew to over one hundred people due to his in-depth Hebraic teaching and the love expressed by the leaders and congregation.

From the beginning of Joey's ministry, he has sought to set people free from bondage and oppression, for the Lord had revealed to him that many were being held hostage by the evil forces, unknown to congregants themselves, and needed to be set free to grow spiritually and be a people without blemish or wrinkle. He and the leaders developed a plan of God, a divine ministry. They named it *Karvenu* (meaning "draw us near"). *Karvenu* is an awakening of our spirit, healing us step-by-step through reflections and impressions, leading us to the path of escape and into freedom and true renewal of our life. My eyes were opened to the heaviness on my shoulders I had throughout my life. I had been stuck in a vicious circle of death and suffering and misery, for the dragon, Satan, had taken hold and was in control of much of my life through one lie after another that I was told, which I came to believe all through the years. This was made known to me while going through my journey in *Karvenu* and subsequence counseling.

> "The thief comes only to steal and kill and destroy; I came that they may have life, and have it abundantly.
> "I am the good shepherd; the good shepherd lays down His life for the sheep. He who is a hired hand, and not a shepherd, who is not the owner of the sheep, sees the wolf coming, and leaves the sheep and flees, and the wolf snatches them and scatters them. He flees because he is a hired hand and is not concerned about the sheep. (John 10:10–13 NASB)

Several times during my life, I sought to kill myself because life seemed unbearable. That was the work of the aggressor (the devil), lying to me through people and circumstances I found myself in. The devil seeks to destroy us. The sheep of the church, including myself, have been scattered time and time again. Many have been deceived as I was. I could not see the truth. I was blinded, and so were they.

> And Jesus said, "For judgment I came into this world, so that those who do not see may see, and that those who see may become blind." (John 9:39 NASB)

When you truly turn to Christ, you begin to see people differently and begin to understand them as you grow in the grace and knowledge of our Lord and Savior Jesus Christ (Yeshua our Messiah). When I was born again, led in the prayer of salvation in Hawaii, I returned back into the darkness from which I came, the same people, the same situation, without seeking the Word of God or any instruction on how to proceed with the rest of my life. I did not lose my salvation but continued in my struggle to live a decent, godly, spirit-filled life. I needed to read and understand the Bible to do so. The evil spirits that were on me (unknown to me then) kept me from seeking Him, from reading the Word of God much of the time. It was a struggle.

Satan and his angels are here on earth right now, roaming around, looking for those whom they may deceive and destroy, and as it says in Revelation 12:19 (NASB), "And the great dragon was thrown down, the serpent of old who is called the devil and Satan, who deceives the whole world; he was thrown down to earth, and his angels were thrown down with him." His mission is to destroy mankind, particularly followers of Christ.

My home was full of these evil spirits that were constantly tormenting me and my spouse, using us against one another. There was much bitterness between us. Bitterness acts in two ways: to defend and/or to comfort ourselves. The devil uses bitterness as strongholds in our life. I was making many inner vows of how I was going to change the future of my life, saying things like, "I am not going to be like my mother." I made rushed judgments on people based on lies I believed. Through *Karvenu*, we (I) learned how to break that stronghold and just what it was over my life. I learned how to protect myself from emotional pain and seek comfort and make the Lord my defense.

His Word, the Bible, had not yet come fully alive to me earlier in my life until I started Bible college in California. Still, there was so much taught that I could not comprehend or utilize in day-to-day living. I learned enough to be dangerous to others in word and deed. There was so much more we all could have received had the leaders really understood or had the full revelation of what they were teaching and if our eyes had been opened. Life continued on for me as usual...a struggle.

> "Behold, the days are coming," declares the Lord
> God, "when I will send a famine on the land, not

a famine for bread or a thirst for water, but rather
for hearing the words of the Lord… They will go
to and fro to seek the word of the Lord, but they
will not find it." (Amos 8:11–12 NASB)

Many people, after years of attending church, become rigid and inflexible and have actually stopped seeking God because they have succumbed to set formulas devised from previous church experiences. Their focus gets stuck on methods and doctrines. They usually feel empty even though they think they are living the complete gospel. They resist change. They resist any move of God because it doesn't meet their own set of standards. They can't hear or understand His Word. They prefer to stay in their miserable comfort zone. How sad!

During 2016 and pursuing years at Sukkat Shalom under Joey Benami's teaching, and specifically in *Karvenu* with Charlotte Barnes, one of our counselors, my eyes were opened, and the scales fell off. I could see! I was able to come to grips with the heaviness and oppression that kept me from being who I was meant to be. Even though I had gone through deliverance a few times in the past for generational curses, there was more they did not discern or comprehend that I needed deliverance from.

We all face different types of problems in life: our job, marriage, our financial situations, debt, too much wealth, medical issues, family relationships, prejudice, unplanned or unwanted pregnancy, and more. When we are in bondage to these so-called burdens, problems, or issues such as I was almost my entire life. We are not able to free ourselves without godly tools and/or knowledge. We need someone on the outside of us sometimes who knows the spiritual forces' attributes to deliver us or lead us through and out of the bondage that has controlled our lives and thinking. We need to know and understand how to keep from being used by that evil force every day of our lives and know the signs of when the adversary is trying to control us again.

For we do not wrestle against flesh and blood,
but against principalities, against powers, against
the rulers of the darkness of this age, against spir-

itual hosts of wickedness in the heavenly places.
(Ephesians 6:12 KJV)

There are many enemy spirits in Satan's arsenal that try to take control through any trauma or tragedy in a person's life, such as sexual violations, controlling or abusing spouse, parental abandonment, rejection from childhood, not ever being good enough, unforgiveness, emotional abuse, physical abuse, and more. This may cause you to not be able to receive healing even from anointed people, although you may get temporary comfort, but it always seems to come back because the enemy's spirit is still present. This may lead to debilitating diseases and suffering from bad or poor health and may cause you to be depressed; feel hopeless; have fibromyalgia, allergies, stomach pain; develop cancer; and even premature death. The Jezebel spirit—along with several other spirits such as Ahab, Orion, and Legion spirits—may come upon you and be the cause of many of your afflictions and burdens you have encountered during your life. Many in congregations around the world are afflicted with these spirits and are completely unaware of it and wonder why they aren't being healed or retaining the spoken and written Word of God. I know this from personal experience. I finally found the way to freedom, and I can praise the Lord for that.

Freedom and unity are sorely needed in our congregations to see and apply the power of God given to us by Yeshua (Jesus) to do the great things He said we would do. There is no unity when you are disturbed by the loudness of music being administered. Wear earplugs. You don't like the food that is being served; bring something you like to share with others. You don't like a particular person in the congregation. Is that person dictating your life? So perhaps you should pray, asking the Lord what bothers you about this person and how you can overcome it. You don't like how the leaders are doing or not doing things for or with the congregation; well, did God put you in charge? Perhaps there is a time or season of discomfort God feels His people must go through to get to another level of growth or understanding or promotion, even if it means taking us into the desert. Be still and receive!

Karvenu literally means "draw us near" to God. It is part of the Freedom Ministry, a tool, a travel journal into the desert of your life produced by Charlotte Barns. The Lord will reveal Himself to you as you interact with Him during the journey, covering lots of ground or territory in your life. Are there soul ties with someone or something in your life? Is there perversion or unhealthy behavior in current or past generations that is being continued in some manner through the behavior of the generations that follow? Were judgments and inner vows of shame directed toward you? Have you had emotional wounds of the soul caused by your father or mother or even a spouse, causing issues with your identity? Do you feel a heavy weight on you that you cannot explain?

During my journey in *Karvenu*, I discerned the skeletons (spirits) of my ancestors hidden within the closets of life past and how they operate in a person's life, my life today. I certainly had some of these spirits on me to various degrees, if not all of them, and I was able to identify other people I had to deal with in my past who were carrying and operating through some of these spirits. Awareness and knowledge of how to deal with these spirits are crucial to being completely healed and set free. How wonderful that even in my old age, I was able to be set free and enjoy the remainder of my years without all the turmoil and suffering of my former years. Glory be to God!

Now I have the full picture. The devil does not want you to see the full picture. He does not want you to be free. He is afraid if you have the whole picture, you will be set free, and he will no longer have a hold on you to do his work. Through Sukkat Shalom and *Karvenu*, my life has changed for the better. Your life can change for the better if you honestly and fervently seek to change the circumstances in your life. The devil wants to keep you in bondage to serve him. *You are either in agreement with God*, or you are in agreement with the devil. There is no in-between!

When your eyes are opened to what has held you, you will be able to understand and know how to be set free to receive God's inner healing and freedom from oppression and bondage. I have now found peace and tranquility in my home, enjoying all that the *Lord Jesus* has given me. So thankful am I that He hears me and that I can hear His still, small voice within me, thankful that the Holy Spirit leads and directs me every day. I have the victory and rejoice in His healing every day, and for the rest of my life shall I honor Him.

Forgiveness

To some the words *forgiveness, forgive, forgiving* are just a figure of speech or a word *Christians* and others use. Many people do not know they are carrying unforgiveness. Oh, they may have said those words "I forgive" nonchalantly but still harbor resentment and anger. If the anger or resentment is not dealt with, it stays inside a person and begins to rot. It ferments and brings sickness, disease (which many people suffer from), and death. You must let go of the infection, not put a Band-Aid on it. You must make a conscious decision to let it go and pray for a new heart to come in and replace your scarred heart. Ask the Lord to bless the person who caused the hurt or abuse. It may be only empty words at first, but God hears you and will help you through it (Matthew 6:14–15 NASB).

Many have followed false teachings like, "You need to bury it," as I had on forgiveness and had never been set free. Forgiveness is letting go of your right to continue to accuse a person, to let God seek revenge that may be due and make the judgments and you not seeking revenge. It is *not* burying or denying the hurt or the injustice committed to you or others as some preachers proclaim and teach. Forgiveness actually slams the door on the enemy and allows you to be healed completely *if* that is what you truly want and seek.

You are encouraged to ask the Lord, our Redeemer and Savior, what you should do. I encourage you to ask Him if you have anything you may need to be delivered from. You say you can't hear His voice. Perhaps Satan is not allowing you to hear His voice so he can continue using you for his purposes. So what then? Keep reading, and I will tell you.

The wounding behaviors that I had to endure from the time I was conceived to old age from parents, grandparents, spouses, my daughter and grandchildren, church members, pastors, coworkers, police officers, doctors, counselors, and others affected my entire life. I was kept in bondage by the adversary, Satan. My father and mother were not present, not emotionally connected to me or the family, and brought strong feelings of being rejected and abandoned by them, never being good enough no matter what I did for them or others.

Behind closed doors, my grandparents were harsh and controlling but were impostors in public view. There was no unconditional love shown, and I was always reminded of my mistakes, being just like my mother, which brought condemnation.

None of my parents were truly caring, loving, kind, or forgiving. They lived in denial and fear, nor did they respect each other.

There was no decision-making for me to do, for it was not allowed or accepted. No words of affirmation or encouragement were spoken over me or to me. I was rejected in the womb from the very beginning and was almost aborted then wished they had when I turned out to be a girl and *not* a boy.

I was emotionally abused by parents by their yelling, screaming, berating and extreme control, physically and sexually abused by grandparents, spouses, bosses, pastors and others who fractured my self-esteem and my ability to function as a normal human being. The sexual incest, molestation, and rapes from family members took their toll on me. If any of this sounds familiar to you, you need to be set free!

My mother was my example as an abused, unloved, unforgiven, worthless, shameful, rejected, brokenhearted woman, according to her parents. To me she was the "norm" for my life. Being far from perfect, I did and said many hurtful, shameful things to others through my life.

Wherever your thoughts take you, your emotional state or mind naturally follows close behind. When your thoughts are on the burden, your emotional state carries that problem. When you mind concerns itself with the things of the heart, the childlike heart, it will respond by maturing little by little and becomes more in tune to the things of God. In other words, be mindful; think about what you are about to speak out. Proverbs 18:4 (NASB) says, "The words of a man's mouth are deep waters; the fountain of wisdom is a bubbling brook." Therefore, hold fast to the Word of God, I have to remind myself often.

All those behaviors and situations growing up and early adult life gave the enemy access through my much-wounded heart and soul (even though it was no fault of my own). Many times, I was tempted to do evil and fell into the sin of that temptation, but that was a choice I made, not the devil. The enemy was permitted to attach himself to me due to severe pain, anger, and resulting bitterness that came about throughout childhood and young adult years. This allowed the enemy to walk in and literally take residence, even develop a stronghold of enemy territory that caused a lifetime of strife with men, women, relationships, spouses, and my daughter and her children.

I suffered from *fear, anxiety, rejection, abandonment, shame, anger, depression, jealousy, pride, death,* and *hopelessness* almost my entire life. The evil spirits made me feel as if I had been stabbed over and over in my heart, like I was bleeding inside and asking the Lord to let me die. I had no security or protection that I could detect from people. It was as though I was in mourning, grieving much of my childhood and adult life. Those who raised me failed me. The church leadership failed me. My spouses failed me, and my employers in the workplace failed me. Adult and child protective services failed me. Medical doctors failed me. Does any of this sound like your life?

Automatically, I was determined to make all wrongs right, particularly in the workplace. I exposed wrongdoings of all kinds of leaders and management in many of my jobs by reporting them to those higher in the chain of command. Sometimes I wonder if this was out of trusted emotions from hurts or me simply wanting to see good come of people. This led me to being shamed, slammed, and fired or forced to quit, further causing rejection and bitterness. Yet I realize God may have been working through me for good. To this day, I stand by Ephesians 5:11–13 (NASB):

> Do not participate in the unfruitful deeds of darkness, but instead even expose them; for it is disgraceful even to speak of the things which are

done by them in secret. But all things become visible when they are exposed by the light, for everything that becomes visible is light.

People will try to define me by my mistakes. We can go through one or more bad seasons or make one or more mistakes, but I can't let that error condemn me or put labels on me. I am defined by what God says I am. *I am a child of God. I am covered by God's blood, mercy, and love. He has redeemed me and given me life everlasting. He has forgiven me and makes me new every morning.* He removes all labels (lies) the enemy and the world put on me. No matter that I made many mistakes, I am not a failure. I am not disqualified. God kept picking me up and allowing me to start over again because He loves me. What we all need is *love*, which God gives freely.

Sadly and most unfortunately, many inside the church and outside the church would rather keep the security of their bondage, their known miserable life, than to go after freedom and truly live the abundant life God offers them, doing His will. It looks too impossible for most in their current circumstances. Pressing in to God or allowing ourselves to follow the Holy Spirit may lead us to a dry area, a wilderness for a time. But when we get to the other side of that wilderness, you will find fulfillment, abundant life, victory, and joy in the Lord, just as I did. No regrets!

As I come to the end of writing this book, I find myself still in a global pandemic called coronavirus or COVID-19. Fear is ramped as is rebellion and unbelief in many around the world. Before this virus was proclaimed, I was suffering from severe pain and numbness in my arms and hands, injury from a bad fall I had in October 2018, which hindered any further writing of this book unless I took action to resolve the problem.

One particular neurosurgeon in Fort Worth, whom the Lord led me to, discovered I had a severely slipped disc in my neck that would cause me to become paralyzed unless it was surgically removed and replaced with a small medical cage and plate holding it in place. Immediately, surgery was done, and it successfully stopped the level-10 pain I was having for a while.

He also discovered I needed to wait for surgery on my lumbar due to severe osteoporosis. I started taking injections daily to build up by bones. Three weeks later, I had severe pain in my chest, and my daughter rushed me to the ER, where I was admitted for pneumonia and mastitis (at age seventy-eight) for four days and was heavily medicated. The X-rays, CT scan, and MRI found a mass in one lung and a lump in my breast.

My daughter was allowed to stay with me the entire four days, and then I was discharged with no medications. I knew in my heart this was another attempt of Satan to disquiet me. Even so, fear of pain fell on me. Five days later, I was back in the ER for pain in my chest and my heart rate racing. They diagnosed an abnormal heart rhythm called atrial fibrillation and kept me for another three days, but this time, due to COVID-19, they would not allow my daughter to go past the emergency room door of the hospital. I felt alone even knowing God, Yeshua, and the Holy Spirit were there with me.

Then I was discharged without medication again. This made me mad, for I knew better. After years of abuse, I still fell into the trap of being a victim until I remembered the prayer, "My God is the rock of my pain in times of trouble and a refuge for me when I call upon Him."

The Word of God and His still, small voice reassured me that He was still in charge and would see me through whatever the devil throws at me. About six visits to ER, including two more stays in the hospital with pneumonia and with resolve of having asthma now, I knew my life was in Jesus's (Yeshua my Redeemer) hands, and no matter what the issues truly are, my faith in Him will bring victory to me. To continue with doctor appointments, I've had to get tested for the coronavirus, just as millions of people have been tested. The results were negative. I can see myself completely healed. *Faith in God* is the best medication and knowing His Word. Just as I am typing this sentence, I got a call from my breast surgeon, who said the biopsy that was done a few days ago found cancer, and I need to have surgery ASAP. I am telling you to stay strong without wavering! I am an overcomer. *We have the victory in Him!*

Because of COVID-19, most churches were closed for a while in 2020 and 2021. People stayed home and got used to staying home out of comfort and many out fear of venturing out. Some ordained people in the church and some of the laypeople of various ministries decided to open their own ministry in their homes or elsewhere and did not return to their congregations. Many watch services now online. Some in the congregation that was attending watch services at www.SukkatShalom.US in Arlington, Texas.

The ministry called *Karvenu* is now renamed Defining Freedom with Charlotte Barnes, who is a certified life coach with a degree in bachelor of biblical counseling. She has her own ministry now apart from Sukkat Shalom Congregation and can be reached in Texas at DefiningFreedom@DefiningFreedom.org. She is majorly responsible for counseling me and helping me and others through the *Karvenu* sessions and for loaning me her book entitled *Restored to Freedom* by Nelson L. Schuman, which after reading it, I ordered my very own book and went through every page with a fine-tooth comb several times even though I did the exercises victoriously the first time I read it. I continue to use this book and my *Karvenu* materials as reference. Sukkat Shalom Congregation is still active and well, and Joey Benami is conducting services on the Shabbat (Saturdays). He is an excellent teacher of Old and New Testaments, particularly with Leviticus in the Old Testament, making it exciting to hear the Word for our lives today.

After having surgery to remove breast cancer, I had surgery on both eyes called bilateral upper lid blepharoplasty, causing me to look like Frankenstein for several weeks. I can laugh about it now, but it wasn't so funny at the time. Once I was recovered from that, the pain in both my arms and hands got to a level 9 again, and I could not handle it anymore. Pain pills seem to do nothing for me, so I ended up having carpal tunnel surgery on both wrists, rendering me unable to clothe or feed myself for over a week. Thank the Lord for grandchildren who came and helped me, even feeding me. The year 2020 ended in victory for me, and I am extremely happy that the Lord is healing my spirit, soul, and body and that I feel like a new person.

Through all that happened to me, I learned to appreciate everything I have, what the Lord has given to me and done for me. I feel like a very rich person even though I have little in the world's eyes. Amassing money or possessions doesn't make you rich or happy, only perhaps comfortable for a time. Doing what you love and having the ability to do it regardless of how much or little you earn from it are truly a blessing from God. I thank Him from the bottom of my heart for all He has done. I am blessed!

The Lord is always there to hear you and is quick to respond. If you say or believe, "He doesn't talk to me," perhaps that is an indication there is a spiritual block from the enemy, not allowing you or wanting you to hear the Lord. Drawing near to the Lord and counseling with qualified, knowledgeable counselors who understand how evil spirits control people will open your eyes to obstacles in your path. You will learn how to deal with evil spirits and negative people. Allow yourself to become the person God created you to be. God loves you, so love yourself. Choose life, not death!

Let God lead you through the barren areas of your life and into the promised life that He has for you. Are you ready? Seek Him and you will find Him and the true self you were meant to be. Seek the Lord with all your heart and you will find Him and be set free. *Receive your freedom!*

> I love the Lord, for he heard my voice; he heard my cry for mercy. Because he turned his ear to me, I will call on him as long as I live.
> The cords of death entangled me, the anguish of the grave came over me; I was overcome by distress and sorrow.
> Then I called on the name of the Lord: "Lord save me!"
> The Lord is gracious and righteous; our God is full of compassion. The Lord protects the unwary; when I was brought low, he saved me.
> Return to your rest, my soul, for the Lord has been good to you. For you Lord, have delivered

me from death, my eyes from tears, my feet from stumbling, that I may walk before the Lord in the land of the living. (Psalm 116:1–9 NIV)

May God bless you.

ABOUT THE AUTHOR

Writing in a journal every day as an adult helped Irene to cope with trials and tribulations in her life. Then one day in 1973, Irene heard the Lord telling her she should write a book telling the story of her life. She laughed about it, not believing she could actually do such a thing.

As the years went by, she came across so many people who needed help just as she was experiencing herself. In her efforts to help others, she realized she did not have the knowledge or tools even to help herself, let alone helping hurting, hopeless people. It wasn't until around 2005 while working as a licensed real estate agent that she took the Lord seriously. She started turning her journals and life experiences into a book.

Her desire is to encourage abused, hopeless people to find their purpose in life and to instruct and inspire them to develop skills to be productive in society and find their spiritual walk. Her belief is no matter what trials we go through, there is always a way out for those who trust in the Lord. It just takes courage and the will to change. Now as a retired businesswoman, Irene is able to enjoy life to the fullest with the guidance and direction of the Lord.

Printed in the USA
CPSIA information can be obtained
at www.ICGtesting.com
LVHW042327140724
785503LV00006B/128

9 798890 612229